DUBLIN
AND THE
VIKING WORLD

Howard B. Clarke,

Sheila Dooley and Ruth Johnson

THE O'BRIEN PRESS

DUBLIN

First published 2018 by The O'Brien Press Ltd,
12 Terenure Road East, Rathgar, Dublin 6, D06 HD27, Ireland.
Tel: +353 1 4923333; Fax: +353 1 4922777
E-mail: books@obrien.ie. Website: www.obrien.ie
The O'Brien Press is a member of Publishing Ireland.

ISBN: 978-1-78849-016-0

8 7 6 5 4 3 2 1
22 21 20 19 18

Printed by EDELVIVES, Spain.
The paper in this book is produced using pulp from managed forests.

Book design, book cover design and typesetting: Anú Design, Tara

Cover: (top) detail of panel depicting Brian Bórama addressing his army before the Battle of Clontarf, courtesy of City Hall Dublin/Dublin City Council; (bottom) replica ship *Havhingsten fra Glendalough* (*The Sea Stallion from Glendalough*), courtesy of Werner Karrasch/Viking Ship Museum, Roskilde; (corners) detail of gilt silver brooch from Rinkaby, Sweden, courtesy of Katarina Nimmervoll/The Swedish History Museum.

Published in

DUBLIN
UNESCO
City of Literature

DUBLINIA
EXPERIENCE VIKING AND MEDIEVAL DUBLIN

Funded by Dublinia, an independent, not-for-profit organisation, dedicated to Dublin's Viking and Medieval past.

Contents

Acknowledgements

The Medieval Trust, the parent body of Dublinia Ltd, is a charitable company established for educational and research purposes. Any profits are reinvested to those ends and the authors wish first to acknowledge a generous financial contribution towards the costs of production. The visitor centre at Dublinia is intended for Dubliners and visitors alike and the same goes for this book. We wish also to thank Denise Brophy, the director of Dublinia, for her enthusiastic support for this project from its inception.

This book is very much the result of teamwork at The O'Brien Press and we are particularly grateful to Michael O'Brien, its founder, for his deep sense of personal commitment and valuable comments on the draft text. Our editor, Aoife Walsh, has displayed impressive professionalism in dealing with the numerous complexities, not the least of which was a trio of co-authors. In addition, Matthew Parkinson-Bennett was responsible for much insightful copy-editing at an earlier stage. The team at Anú Design have achieved amazing creativity in their ideas for layout, taking advantage of the wonders of Viking Age artistry.

A special word should be said about maps. The Viking world was not made up of nation states. Europe was still in a condition of political flux and formation, as it would remain for many centuries to come. Vikings participated in that formative process and famously, of course, their descendants did so more permanently on foot of winning a dramatic battle near Hastings in the year 1066. For charting a cartographical path through all of this, we thank Terry Foley for his standardised versions of existing maps taken from a variety of sources.

Finally we are grateful to all of those individuals and institutions that willingly gave us permission to reproduce illustrative materials and to Mary Robinson for her foreword.

Foreword

This excellent book is an ideal way to mark the 25th anniversary year of *Dublinia*, Dublin's heritage centre and museum located at Christ Church, the crossroads of the medieval city. And right next door to what was once one of Europe's largest urban archaeological sites, Wood Quay.

My introduction to Dublin's role in the Viking world was back in the 1970s when I acted as legal counsel for Fr F.X. Martin, Professor of Medieval History at University College Dublin and Chairman of the Friends of Medieval Dublin. Dismayed at the city fathers' decision to bulldoze the Wood Quay site, where the original ninth-century Viking settlement of the city lay beneath the

contemporary city, Fr Martin and the Friends came together to inspire and lead an extraordinary civic movement to try to protect the site. They succeeded in delaying the destruction of the site for eight years – valuable time for archaeological excavation.

Sadly, the dream of preserving the Viking site and old city walls disappeared. But today, Dublin's Viking legacy is kept alive through *Dublinia*, which displays a fraction of the thousands of artefacts recovered and stored by the National Museum of Ireland, as well as items from the far-flung Viking world. It is so valuable to learn about the lifestyle and activities of the time such as leather and cloth production, barrel-making, toys, houses and combs made from wood and bone. Sights, sounds and smells of the city are all vividly represented in the exhibition.

Howard Clarke, a founder member of the Friends of Medieval Dublin, Sheila Dooley, former curator and educational officer in *Dublinia*, and Ruth Johnson, the city archaeologist for Dublin City Council, have produced a well-researched, understandable and entertaining read – and a welcome visual experience of the Viking age. The book presents readers with many different and enriching insights into the reality of daily life in Viking Dublin over a thousand years ago. At that time Dublin was a multilingual town with both Old Norse and Irish languages being spoken on a daily basis. While Viking raids were the necessary and often traumatic precursor to settlement, widespread for a period before that, it's interesting to learn how all the peoples of Viking Dublin evolved towards a multicultural society – something which has resonance for us today.

More than anything *Dublinia* and this book help us to understand how we have been shaped as a people and a culture and to strengthen our sense of identity.

Mary Robinson
(President of Ireland, 1990–1997)

Preface

The Dublinia exhibition at Christ Church opened its doors to the public in 1993, focusing on the high and late Middle Ages. Its story began with the capture of Dublin by Anglo-Norman warriors allied to the king of Leinster, Diarmait Mac Murchada, in 1170; it ended with the beginning of the Protestant Reformation *c.* 1540. This is the story of an already established town that was colonised and developed further by foreigners whose background lay in southern Britain and northern France.

By stages a new and historically earlier story was added to the exhibition, focused on the Viking phase of the city's origin. Over the years, this has proved to be a popular draw to visitors, whose numbers have increased dramatically. The early medieval period (*c.* 400 to *c.* 1000), which includes most of the Viking Age, has fewer written records and scholars have a correspondingly greater dependence on archaeology. Accordingly a substantial archaeological display was installed on the exhibition's top floor.

A natural outcome of these developments is this book, devoted to Dublin before 1170. It has been designed in much the same way as *Dublinia: The Story of Medieval Dublin*, which was published in 2002. As before, it will be of particular interest to visitors and readers who like to engage with archaeology, history and historical

Left: Dublinia is housed in a listed building that was opened for Church of Ireland synods in 1875. The historic tower of St Michael's medieval church is subsumed within the building, from which breathtaking views of Dublin can be admired.

Right: Dublinia heritage centre facing north. Its unique and engaging exhibitions have inspired millions of visitors since opening in 1993. Promoting the unique heritage of Dublin in an accurate and inclusive way, it has become one of Dublin's 'must-see' attractions.

geography. Above all, of course, there is the enduring allure of those other foreigners whose background lay in Scandinavia – the Vikings.

The Wood Quay archaeological site between Christ Church Cathedral and the River Liffey. This photograph demonstrates years of slow, meticulous searching that exposed many aspects of the lifestyle and history of Viking Dublin. Thousands of discovered artefacts are now displayed or stored in the National Museum of Ireland. Eventually, the site was bulldozed and the ancient city wall partially removed to make way for Dublin's civic offices.

Viking Dublin will always be associated with the campaign spearheaded by the Friends of Medieval Dublin and led by F.X. Martin, OSA in the late 1970s and early 1980s, the aim of which was to preserve archaeological remains from the Middle Ages, including the Viking Age, at Wood Quay. Though the site was eventually bulldozed, much invaluable material was recovered for posterity. Had not this recovery been the case, significant parts of this book could never have been written.

Older readers will recall what became known, with entirely apposite irony, as the Wood Quay Saga. Dublin Corporation had planned to build multi-million-pound tower blocks as civic offices on the 4½ acre site between Christ Church Cathedral and the River Liffey. Their construction provoked a dramatic confrontation between those who wanted to maintain the site as a national monument and a bureaucratic machine determined to get its way at any cost.

Archaeological investigations had already demonstrated that this was a site of international, as well as national, importance. Structural foundations and individual artefacts were found to be in an excellent state of preservation. When the remaining layers were threated by bulldozing in 1977, the Friends of Medieval Dublin pursued court action. The most dramatic incident occurred in June 1979 when twenty prominent citizens of Ireland occupied the site and stopped the building works for twenty-one days.

In the end a preservation clause in the 1930 National Monuments Act was used opportunistically by the corporation, backed by the national government, to 'demolish' the site. Two of the four proposed tower blocks, popularly known as the civic bunkers, still stand today as architectural reminders of these events. More positively, another eventual outcome was the appointment in 1991 of Dublin's first city archaeologist. That position, still fiercely challenging, ensures constant monitoring of archaeological issues as they arise. It is a position, too, that is held today by one of the authors of this book, Ruth Johnson.

Introduction

Dublin and the Viking World aims to introduce readers to the period when Dublin became Ireland's first fully functioning town. It is a blend of the familiar and the unfamiliar, the broad generalisation and the rarefied detail, the well-known historical character and the ordinary Dubliner of past times. The primary focus is on Dublin and its immediate hinterland, but throughout this book the wider world inhabited by Vikings is never far away.

In the Viking world a person who was tempted to 'ransack' (Old Norse *rannsaka*) someone's house might then be declared an 'outlaw' (Old Norse *útlagi*) by way of punishment. Thousands of other English words, some very basic such as 'leg' (*leggr*) and 'skin' (*skinn*) and others more localised, are either direct borrowings from Old Norse – the language of the Vikings – or they have been influenced in their spelling by contact with Old Norse. To take a single example, Old English as spoken by the Anglo-Saxon people of early medieval England contains the word *frēond* meaning 'friend', but the modern spelling is nearer to Old Norse *frændi*, which also has connotations of kinship.

Our main text is divided into ten short chapters, each dealing with a major theme. Chapters 1 and 9 establish the chronological limits of the Viking Age as extending from *c.* 790 to *c.* 1100. In practice there are differences of historical opinion about this question, partly because of variations in the experiences of the peoples of Europe, including the Scandinavians themselves. Another factor is that many archaeologists refer to a late Viking Age that includes much of the twelfth century as well. At the very least, the dating range adopted here suits the Irish experience perfectly.

Chapters 3 and 4 focus on the three principal activities associated with Vikings – raiding, trading and settling. These are different processes, of course, and they varied in intensity and in their long-term consequences. In the case of Ireland, raiding by Viking warriors was a relatively widespread experience, especially in the ninth and tenth centuries, whereas permanent settlement was limited for the most part to a small number of coastal trading settlements and their immediate hinterlands.

Chapters 5 and 6 bring the reader into the world of craft-working and the homestead. As in other contemporary cultures, Scandinavians of the Viking Age, whether in their homelands or abroad, spent most of their lives engaged in survival skills to acquire food, clothing and shelter, and in the business of making useful things from the plants, metals and animals that they acquired. No physically fit person was unemployed; the Viking world was a world of work.

Artist's impression of Viking Dublin *c.* 975. Features to note are the earth and timber defences, the royal compound on the site of the later castle, the pool sheltering the fleet and trading activity on the bank of the Liffey.

Map of the Viking world. Dublin in Ireland and York in England were central to that world. Archaeological finds in Dublin have been linked to L'Anse aux Meadows in Newfoundland in the west and to Novgorod in northern Russia in the east.

The subject of Dublin raises the question of what Viking towns were like, which is touched on in Chapter 7. Scholars differ profoundly in how they approach this topic, partly because urban origins themselves were so varied. Different historical processes led to the emergence and development of town life. Dublin is an example of a trading settlement that came to acquire by stages – often hesitant ones – the character of what might reasonably be regarded as a town. Whatever definition we may prefer as to what constituted a 'town', there is no doubt that in the case of Dublin it was a process and not an event.

When Vikings started to make contact with a Christian country such as Ireland, one of their most striking cultural manifestations was their Nordic paganism. Irish annalists called them Gentiles, a biblical term for people with a different set of religious beliefs. Chapter 8 explores this topic, together with the intriguing question of how paganism and Christianity coexisted before, in the

late Viking Age, the foreigners themselves chose, or were persuaded, to adopt the faith of the local population.

Finally we look at some aspects of what is called the Viking legacy in Chapter 10. In today's world, Vikings are in a certain sense alive and well; they enjoy enduring appeal. Books about them are written and films of Viking derring-do have become popular. With little historical justification, the horned helmet has become a symbol of being a Viking. In Ireland, 'Vikings' even participate in St Patrick's Day processions.

As an archaeological site is being excavated, small finds are customarily placed in a box before being taken away for analysis and conservation. In this book we have used 'Finds Box' sections to highlight the sorts of evidence that emerge in the course of archaeological excavations. Readers will be able to compare the contribution of archaeology with that of conventional written records. One important difference that should always be borne in mind is that archaeological dating tends to be less specific than historical dating.

One of the most impressive legacies of the Viking world is the enormous body of saga literature produced later on, mainly in Iceland. These written sagas were based on the earlier, orally transmitted stories of the Vikings. The general view among scholars is that, while sagas are a type of literature, they do contain nuggets of historical truth. Certainly many of the people in these stories did exist, just like Shakespeare's historical characters. The language of the sagas is Old Norse, the language spoken by the Vikings themselves.

You are about to enter the real Viking world.

Left: Illustrations from the fourteenth-century collection of Icelandic sagas, the Flateyjarbók. This enormous manuscript illuminates the legendary exploits of Norwegian kings, including Óláfr Tryggvason killing a boar and an ogress. He was related by marriage to Dublin's ruling family.

Right: Archaeologists working on a commercial excavation in Dublin city centre. A legally supported zone of archaeological potential means that developers wishing to build there must collaborate with archaeologists to record and, if possible, preserve material remains from the past.

1
The Beginning of the Viking Age

*Archaeologists and historians differ from
one another in their approach, but in the case of Ireland
there is general agreement that the
Viking Age began in the 790s AD*

Nobody in the ninth, tenth and eleventh centuries thought of
themselves as living in the Viking Age, which is essentially an
academic construct. It is part of what Renaissance scholars in
the mid-fifteenth century began to envisage as a 'middle age'

(from Latin *medium ævum*) between the fall of the Roman Empire and their own 'modern' times. Today of course we, too, think of ourselves as living in modern times: 'modern' is a relative term when applied to historical contexts.

A special occurrence during the Viking Age was the passing of the first millennium AD. An English monk named Byrhtferth addressed his contemporaries as 'we who have progressed through the last part of the millennium and beyond'. The millennium of Christ's birth in the year 1000 was a talking point, just as it was in the year 2000, and its successful completion something of a relief. How much more would this have been the case when marauding Vikings were still an everyday threat!

The Norwegian Homeland

Most of the Vikings who raided, traded and settled in Ireland came from the country that we call Norway. Norway is dramatically mountainous with an average altitude of about 500 m above sea level. Towards the west, the mountains form a great plateau, treeless on top but forested lower down, deeply etched by valleys and fjords. South-western Norway is particularly isolated from the rest of the country, whereas in the south-east there is one principal fjord, now called Oslofjord, whose medieval name was Víken, 'the inlet'.

The Norwegian name for the country, *Norge*, is derived from 'north way', which shows that the country was distinguished as a trade route. By the ninth century the English were calling the inhabitants 'northwaymen'. Given the difficulty of overland communications, the lack of sea ice in winter and a wealth of timber, boat- and ship-building were both natural and necessary for the people of Norway. Although the rivers were barely navigable, the fjords were ideal for

Lovatnet Lake, leading to a fjord in western Norway. Deep, smooth water is surrounded by steep, ice-cut hillsides, forested slopes and a small amount of farmable land. Even in summer, mountain tops can still be streaked with snow.

Map showing the territories and trading routes of the Norse population in Viking Age Scandinavia. Danes controlled the Oslofjord region in south-eastern Norway in the ninth century and part of south-western Sweden for many centuries. Norway was especially difficult to unite under a single kingship because of its terrain.

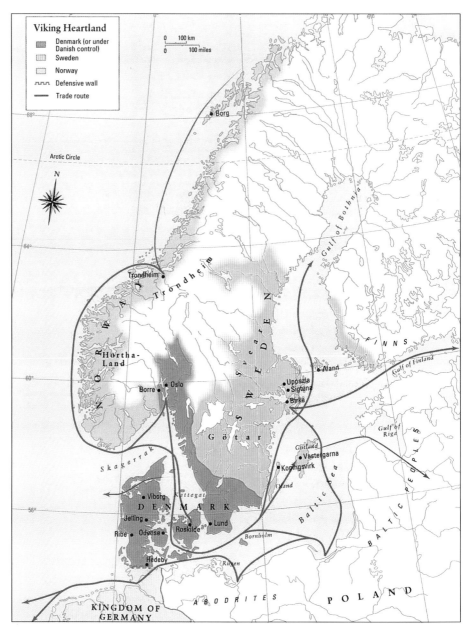

travel and a belt of small islands along the Atlantic coastline gave a degree of shelter, except in the south-west. With proficiency at sea long established and a difficult border with Sweden to the east, the natural direction of expansion overseas was to the west and south-west.

At present about 2.5 percent of Norway is cultivated as arable land, twenty-five percent is forested and the rest is used for high grazing or barren. In the

18

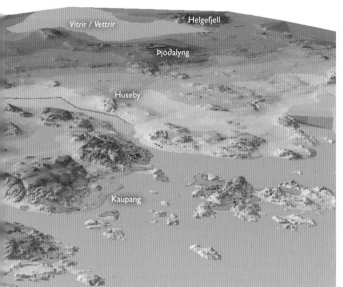

past, the area suitable for agriculture, especially field cultivation, was more limited and not easily extended. Most farmland consisted of narrow strips along fjords, in glaciated valley bottoms and on islands offshore. The balance between sufficiency and population was finely tuned; when there was an excess of people, this compelled migration to elsewhere in Scandinavia or farther afield. For some, the choice was to stay and starve or leave and find sustenance elsewhere.

In terms of farming, the western side of Oslofjord, known as Vestfold, was the best endowed and the richest families were based there. The main ruling dynasty is of uncertain origin, but the most spectacular evidence of prosperity in Norway in the early Viking Age consists of the Oseberg and Gokstad ship burials and the trading settlement at Kaupang. For much of the ninth century, it is now believed, this territory was under Danish overlordship.

Norway, then, offered limited prospects for creating and enjoying wealth. The geographical make-up of Norway made political fragmentation the norm and there were numerous chieftains and even kings in the early Viking Age. Hill-forts reflect this subdivision of social and political power. In western Norway (Vestland) in particular, warrior chieftains held sway over a farming population. Saleable goods were in short supply and there was an inclination to plunder other people's wealth, especially outside Scandinavia. Even young men who came from relatively secure backgrounds were encouraged by their fathers to test their manhood by going on a *víking*, 'freebooting voyage'.

Left: Reconstruction of the site of Kaupang in Vestfold, Norway. Like Dublin, this was a waterside trading settlement surrounded by cemeteries. Men from both the main settlement and the surrounding district assembled for public business at Þjóðalyng, as at Dublin's Þingmót or assembly mound.

Right: The Oseberg ship, buried in Vestfold, Norway, in 834. The early date of this richly decorated vessel makes it an important witness to Scandinavian supremacy in ship design. Both skeletons found in the ship were females, one of high social status.

What was a Viking?

The Old Norse word *víkingr* came to be used for a sea pirate from the region that we call Scandinavia, comprising the modern states of Denmark, Norway and Sweden. It is not certain where this word came from, although it may be connected with the word *vík*, meaning a small creek, inlet or bay. The verb *víkja*, 'to move' or 'to turn', was sometimes used of a ship veering round, and one theory is that a *víkingr* was a person who waited in an inlet before pirating a passing ship.

An alternative view is that the word originally denoted a trader from Víken (Oslofjord) in southern Norway. If some of them occasionally engaged in raiding as well as trading, then the term might gradually have acquired a new meaning. Strictly speaking, the word 'Viking' should be applied only to those Scandinavians who were sea-pirates, but it is now commonly used to refer to all Scandinavian peoples of the Viking Age and their culture.

THE EXPANSION OF THE
FRANKISH EMPIRE

- Areas conquered by Charlemagne
- Areas under Carolingian influence
- Original Carolingian territory

IRELAND

ENGLAND

DENMARK

Aachen

Rome

N

Map artwork by Anu Design (www.anu-design.ie)

Left: Reconstruction of a Viking Age farm at Avaldsnes in Rogaland. Around the time of his victory at Hafrsfjord, King Haraldr chose as his principal residence Avaldsnes, now the site of a major visitor centre with a longhouse, boathouse and other buildings.

Below: Worked and unworked amber from Fishamble Street, Dublin. Amber is a yellowish fossil resin from pine forests and was particularly plentiful along the south-eastern Baltic coastline. Beads, pendants and rings were fashionable items of jewellery during the Viking Age.

Around the end of the eighth century, so-called Vikings began to leave their Scandinavian homelands. Some were traders exploiting new commercial opportunities as north-western Europe developed economically during the expansive reign of the great Frankish king and emperor, Charles the Great (Charlemagne). Others were farmers in search of good land, especially younger sons who had few or no prospects back home. Yet others were pure opportunists intent on raiding for instant wealth. There was probably no such person as a 'typical' Viking.

Another factor may have been an increasing demand in other parts of Europe for raw materials from Scandinavia itself, notably amber to make jewellery, animal furs for warm clothing and soapstone as a convenient resource for heat-proof cooking vessels. An exceptional piece of written evidence is the account by King Alfred of Wessex in southern England (871–99) of the trading activities of a native of Hálogaland – the northernmost part of Norway famous for the spectacular display of the Aurora Borealis or Northern Lights. Around the year 890 this man, Óttarr, visited the king and told him about his large herd of reindeer and about his life as a trader of walrus ivory, ropes, furs and feathers in exchange for southern goods such as cloth, malt, metalwork and weapons.

Political developments in Norway itself may have had the unintended result of creating Vikings. Traditionally the kingship of King Haraldr Finehair dates from his victory in a naval battle at Hafrsfjord around the year 870. Estates associated with him

were located in Rogaland, south of Bergen in western Norway, but he appears to have pursued a deliberate policy of establishing his power over as much of the country as he could. The initial colonisation of Iceland, starting in the mid-870s, was conducted by political exiles and rebels, some of whom may alternatively have chosen to stay nearer to home and become Vikings.

Contemporary Views of Vikings

The 'popular' image of Vikings comes from non-Scandinavian writings in Latin, Old English (Anglo-Saxon), Old Irish and, to a lesser extent, Arabic, Greek and Russian. Most of these do not survive in contemporary manuscripts but in later copies, with numerous possibilities for error and omission. In the early twelfth century, Ireland produced its own distinctive source devoted to the Viking wars called *Cogadh Gáedhel re Gallaibh*, the 'War of the Irish with the Foreigners'. This is obviously a biased account in favour of Brian Bórama (Brian Boru), the

The runic alphabet in its two forms. The long-twig forms were favoured in Denmark, the short-twig ones in Norway and Sweden. A mixture of both scripts seems to have been typical of runic inscriptions on the Isle of Man.

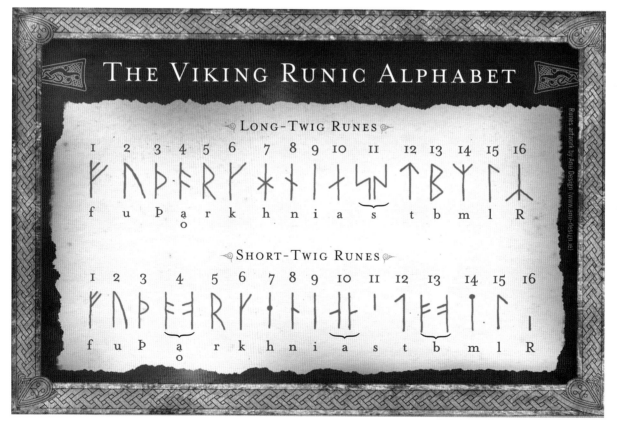

THE VIKING RUNIC ALPHABET

Runes artwork by Anu Design (www.anu-design.ie)

Dublin and the Viking World

upstart king of Munster and high king of Ireland, and his military victory and death in the Battle of Clontarf in 1014.

The only strictly contemporary written evidence for the Viking Age which is of Scandinavian origin consists of runic inscriptions. The runic alphabet was derived from one or more southern European alphabets, especially the Latin one that we ourselves use today. It was designed, like Irish ogham, for incision on wood and stone, with what are called long-twig and short-twig forms. Its limitation to only sixteen letters to represent the entire sound system of Old Norse has led to much difficulty in interpretation. We should nevertheless always bear in mind that some Scandinavians of the Viking Age were literate, yet without any access to books in their own tongue.

Another Scandinavian written source survives only in later manuscripts but is widely believed to reflect contemporary attitudes – a form of poetry known as skaldic verse. It is so named from the Old Norse word *skáld*, 'poet'. A *skáld* was a professional poet, rather like those of Gaelic Ireland in later times, maintained in royal and aristocratic households. These poets invented complex metrical systems, and this kind of verse has come down to us unchanged. Thus we have an accurate impression of the value system of the brave warrior, the firm ruler and the generous patron.

Weapon-brandishing warriors on the Lindisfarne stone. This English monastery was the first in Europe to be attacked by Vikings, in 793. According to the *Anglo-Saxon Chronicle*, 'the ravages of heathen men miserably destroyed God's church … with plunder and slaughter'.

Left: Symbols of the four Evangelists from the Book of Kells. Produced on Iona in western Scotland prior to the first Viking attack, this stunning gospel book was later brought, unfinished, to the monastery at Kells in Ireland.

Right: Life-size figure of a young woman for sale in a slave market, from the Dublinia exhibition. Such women were destined to live as domestic servants and often as concubines.

The Beginning of the Viking Age

Because of their warlike raiding activities, it is inevitable and entirely understandable that western European writers, both churchmen and laymen, portray their Scandinavian contemporaries in a hostile and negative way. Two sorts of violence are recorded. One was violence directed against other people, with the result that an unknown number of men, women and children died at the hands of Vikings. Men fighting in local and national forces to defend their homes and homelands lost their lives or were seriously injured. It is impossible now to estimate the total number of civilian and military casualties. Even more numerous than the dead may have been the male and female slaves captured and sold by Vikings in their joint capacity as raiders and traders.

Violence was also directed against property, again recorded chiefly in annals and chronicles. Towns, villages, hamlets, farmsteads, churches and monasteries all came under Viking attack. The level of material destruction is incalculable and it coexisted with similar destruction occasioned by the locals themselves. Historically the most serious losses may have been books kept in book-shrines, along with libraries such as those at Iona and York. The most famous survivor of Viking mayhem, of course, is the Book of Kells, now safely in Dublin.

Dublin at the Dawn of the Viking Age

One of the standard myths about the history of Dublin is that the place was founded by Vikings. This isn't accurate: Dublin originated as two very different settlements long before the first Viking intrusions. The older of these, still denoted on national road signs in Irish, was Áth Cliath ('ford of hurdle-work'), the site of a major ford across the River Liffey. The ford itself could be crossed by humans and by animals only at low tide, but its strategic position in the system of long-distance highways (Irish *slighte*) would have been one of the attractions of Dublin Bay as a suitable location for a trading settlement.

A second, ecclesiastical settlement had been founded by the middle of the seventh century. It is still defined by its distinctive pear-shaped outline in the present-day Aungier Street area. This may have been the place referred to in annals and martyrologies as Duiblinn (modernised as Dubhlinn), taking its name, meaning 'black pool', from a tidal inlet in the River Poddle a short distance to the north. A number of shadowy personages of early medieval date are described as abbots, bishops and, in one instance, both. Dubhlinn may have

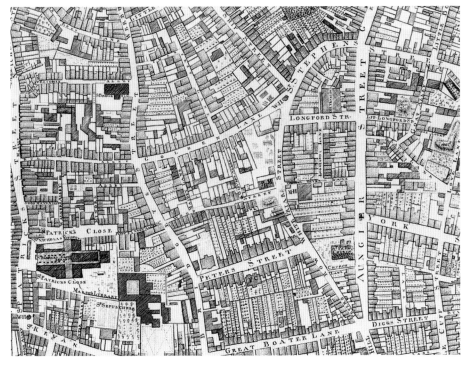

Left: Extract from Rocque's map of Dublin showing the Aungier Street area, 1756. As late as this, and even today, the street pattern preserves the characteristic outline of the early medieval ecclesiastical enclosure of Duiblinn, the 'black pool', that attracted Vikings.

served as the chief church of a small and politically insignificant dynastic group named Uí Fergusa.

Had Vikings been the original founders of Dublin, it would have acquired a Scandinavian name comparable with Waterford and Wexford – both containing the place-name element *fjörðr*, 'fjord' (or 'firth' in Scotland). Instead the foreigners adopted and adapted one of the two existing Irish names in the form Dyflinn and its variants. The precise location of the first Viking settlement, reputedly founded in the year 841, remains uncertain and has been much debated. The most likely scenario is that the monastery on the south side of the pool was seized and its resources commandeered for short-term gain. Some poorly preserved pagan graves have recently been archaeologically excavated in the vicinity along with evidence for early settlement.

After 842, however, most of the annalistic references are to Vikings of Áth Cliath, possibly implying that a second ship harbour (Irish *longphort*) had been established. Some of the invading Norsemen, under the

Below: The head and shoulders of a young adult male found at Ship Street Great, Dublin. This Viking may have been a raider in the Dublin area prior to 841 or even an initial settler. The radiocarbon dating places him here surprisingly early.

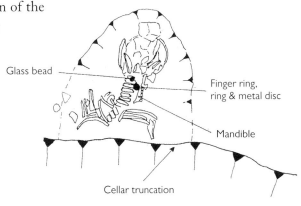

Glass bead

Finger ring, ring & metal disc

Mandible

Cellar truncation

Scale 1:10   m   0.50

Artist's impression of the hurdle ford of Áth Cliath crossing the River Liffey, upstream from the Viking settlement. According to a ninth-century text, this ford was one of the three most important river crossings in Ireland.

Artist's impression of how a late ninth-century sunken-featured building may have looked. Archaeology has revealed a stepped entrance and a cobbled floor. Early Scandinavian settlers in Dublin came from an essentially rural background with no direct experience of town life.

leadership of kings since 853, may have taken advantage of an island in the main river, as they did elsewhere in western Europe in the mid-ninth century. Purely speculatively, Usher's Island could have provided foreign plunderers operating in a hostile environment with a ready-made defensive site that did not require them to construct ditches, ramparts, palisades and gates, none of which has been identified in the archaeological record.

A short distance downstream, at Essex Street West, some evidence of habitation in the second half of the ninth century has been discovered, much of it with rural connotations in the shape of a ploughing level, buildings partly sunk into the ground, wattle enclosures and animal pens. Do these represent the documented *longphort*? In addition a significant number of contemporary 'furnished' pagan burials have been found, notably upstream at Kilmainham and Islandbridge. More archaeological investigation will be required to enable us to understand how this diverse evidence should be interpreted.

At the very least, we can be certain that by the middle of the ninth century Vikings had chosen Dublin as a place to set up home. The tidal pool in the Poddle provided a sheltered haven for their fleet of warships while some sort of quayside may have developed on the Liffey. Raiding and trading, partly ship-based and partly land-based, could be pursued simultaneously and at a profit.

2

Ships and the Sea

The chief weapon of Viking success was their ships; crews of raiders sailed to undefended church sites, attacking them and returning to Norway within a month.

The sea was the raiders' highway to neighbouring settlements, their source of adventure and, at the very least, their source of food. Those who lived by this resource inherited the ability to manipulate it. Boat-builders engineered ship designs never seen prior to the Viking Age using techniques that had been perfected by the eighth century. In Ireland, a complete Viking vessel has yet to be discovered, but fragments of timbers and nails have been uncovered from excavations in Dublin at Fishamble Street, High Street, Wood Quay and John's Lane East. The fragments point to the typical 'clinker'

style of Viking ship-building (overlapping planks rivetted together by nails) being practised in Dublin from around 950 to the twelfth century. The most famed is the late Viking Age long and narrow warship (Old Norse *langskip*), crafted with a strategically shallow draught (water displacement), with room for up to a hundred crew. With this technology, Vikings could access targets via shallow waters and beaches at speed and retreat just as quickly. Naval battles were rare but did occur. Saga accounts refer to ships siding up to each other as fighting platforms, as at the battle of Svold in the year 1000 when the Norwegian king Óláfr Tryggvason was drowned.

Building and Using Ships

The accomplishment of a master ship-builder lay not just in how he built a ship but also in the tools and resources he used to enhance his design. Ship production in the Dublin region concentrated on oak harvested from nearby woodland. Natural curvatures of trees and branches were chosen for specific parts of the ship, while long trunks were crafted into sections for the ship's keel (the backbone of the vessel). Woodsmen split trees with axes rather than sawing them along the natural grain, retaining the wood's innate strength.

A ship's speed and ability to turn relied heavily on a good sailcloth. A relatively small warship (Old Norse *karfi*) such as the early Viking Age Gokstad

Two ships under construction for the Norman invasion fleet in 1066, as shown on the Bayeux Tapestry. The tools being used are adzes, augers and axes, while the horizontal strakes along the sides are emphasised by skilful use of colour.

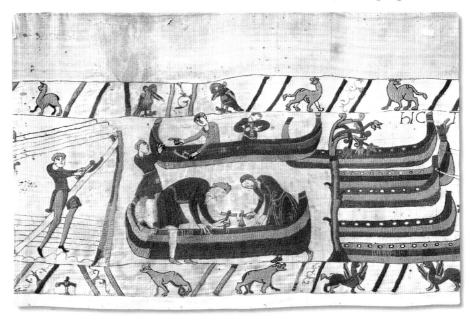

Dublin and the Viking World

HIC TRAHVNT:NAVES:ADMA RE

Newly built ships being launched, by means of ropes drawn round a pole, for the invasion of England. Dragon heads on the prows of warships were not a peculiarly Viking phenomenon. Rows of oarports can also be seen clearly.

ship, holding around thirty-five able-bodied men, could maintain a maximum sailing speed of approximately fifteen knots (about twenty-eight kilometres an hour). A skilled workforce was required to make the sails and this tended to be a female profession. Sheep fleece was processed into yarn to weave squares of wool before they were sewn together by a sailmaker. The wool came from a Norse breed of sheep that populated the Viking world and still grazes today along the coast of Norway. Its double coat contains a high proportion of lanolin, water-repellent wool, making it perfect for use on the high seas. A much larger longship might require a woollen sail weighing about 200 kg, which would need fleece from one hundred sheep to produce.

Painters decorated ships in strong, bright colours. Traces of yellow and black were found on the remains of the Gokstad ship in Vestfold, Norway, while blue, yellow, green and red were discovered on the Ladby ship buried on the island of Funen in Denmark. In Dublin, a ship painter's house was discovered in the archaeological layers of Temple Bar in the city centre. Timbers, including a brightly painted yellow piece from the stern of a clinker-built ship, had been discarded in the back yard. The pigment for creating the colour, orpiment, is not native to Ireland and was manufactured at home; a small amount of it survived along with a stone mortar (bowl-type vessel).

Warships were not the only sea-going vessels built by Scandinavians. Heavier merchant ships (*knörr*, plural *knerrir*) were designed to carry material goods,

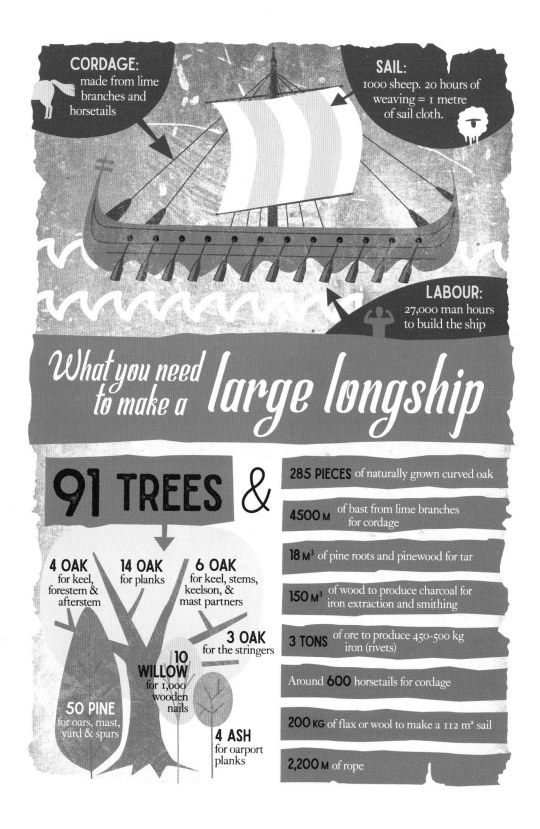

CORDAGE: made from lime branches and horsetails

SAIL: 1000 sheep. 20 hours of weaving = 1 metre of sail cloth.

LABOUR: 27,000 man hours to build the ship

What you need to make a large longship

91 TREES &

4 OAK for keel, forestem & afterstem

14 OAK for planks

6 OAK for keel, stems, keelson, & mast partners

3 OAK for the stringers

10 WILLOW for 1,000 wooden nails

50 PINE for oars, mast, yard & spars

4 ASH for oarport planks

285 PIECES of naturally grown curved oak

4500 M of bast from lime branches for cordage

18 M³ of pine roots and pinewood for tar

150 M³ of wood to produce charcoal for iron extraction and smithing

3 TONS of ore to produce 450-500 kg iron (rivets)

Around **600** horsetails for cordage

200 KG of flax or wool to make a 112 m² sail

2,200 M of rope

including large domestic animals, and could be sailed by as few as six men and transport up to twenty tonnes of cargo. Smaller boats or dug-out canoes were suitable for lakes or rivers and similarly in Celtic Ireland, skin boats or curraghs were being used for fishing and short journeys.

Life on Board Ship

Warriors had to be skilled in battle on land and sometimes on board ship, but also to have the stamina for life at sea. Space was limited: on a late Viking Age longship the distance between each fixed seat (thwart) was about 73 cm, close enough for each crew member to put a hand on a neighbour's shoulder. This space (Old Norse *rúm*) was where the sailors ate, slept and manned the oars on either side of the ship. Skilled oarsmen could power a ship without wind. Even when not rowing, the crew provided ballast and balance, preventing the ship from capsizing in strong winds.

Energy for such work came mainly from eating fruit along with fish or meat that was salted, pickled or smoked to last the journey. Water was carried in skin bags while ale or soured milk was transported in tubs. On the open sea, however, harsh winds, pelting rain and unforgiving cold could create insufferable conditions. There were no basic amenities such as cooking facilities, toilets or beds. Each crew member had a sea-chest where he stored the few belongings he carried with him – a spare item of clothing, a comb, an axe and a whetstone.

At night, the crew slept in the open in a *húðfat* (a word found in several

Left: The Gokstad ship. Built *c*. 890, this vessel was suitable both for raiding and for trading. It was found in a burial mound in the late nineteenth century and is now preserved in the Viking Ship Museum in Oslo.

Right: Warriors with swords and shields in combat and a ship under sail are depicted on a memorial stone from the Swedish island of Gotland. The ship has one centrally placed mast supported by rigging and a large sail made up of squares of fabric sewn together.

The Gokstad ship viewed from near the helmsman's position. With a beam of 5.25 m, this early warship was surprisingly spacious amidships. There were no fixed benches and crew probably sat on their personal sea-chests when taking to the oars.

Left: Bronze-gilt engraved weather-vane from Heggen in Norway, decorated in the late Viking Age Ringerike art style. It was probably mounted originally on the prow of a ship. The Old Norse word *byrr*, found frequently in sagas, meant 'a fair wind'.

Right: Replica of a trading vessel showing its steering board or side rudder and pivot block. All ships in the Viking Age were steered in this way, giving rise in English to the term 'starboard' (meaning 'steering board'), with 'port' on the opposite side.

sagas) – a two-man sleeping-bag made from animal skin – or they were covered by a hide blanket. For higher-status Vikings, shelter may have been provided under collapsible tents. Sailors were positioned around the ship to perform different duties. The helmsman and his closest officers were in the stern, the crew occupied the main part of the ship and the prow was where the sailing tack was stored.

Despite having the best position on a ship, a lookout could not always prevent the crew from the potentially fatal risk of getting lost. Navigators relied on oral traditions recalling the shapes of cliffs, rock formations and island positions.

A starry night sky might assist direction, but for Vikings travelling in nearly twenty-four hours of northern daylight in summertime, birds as natural land detectors could indicate the closest direction to land. Cloud formations, driftwood and ice-glare in the sky were all clues to the whereabouts of land, even when it lay beyond the horizon.

Part of a sun compass of spruce or larch from the Eastern Settlement, Greenland, c. 1000. A reconstruction of such a compass features thirty-two points, the central gnomon to create a shadow, and other markings related to the time of year.

Seasonal Raids

'Make your ship ready for the sea when the summer starts, and navigate in the best part of summer … and do not stay on the sea in the autumn if you can help it.' So says the *King's Mirror*, a book of advice from a Norwegian to his son written much later in the thirteenth century.

Monasteries were vulnerable and easily accessible sources of food, horses, valuable religious relics deposited by local Irish dynasts, and hostages for ransom or the slave market. Ambitious minor kings and wealthy chieftains in Norway and Denmark sponsored expeditions to these monasteries, commissioning ships, crews and material resources to raid overseas. A journey from Norway to Ireland, a distance of roughly 1,350 km, might take around a week in good weather and include a pit-stop to restock on the Shetland Islands, halfway between Norway and the Orkney Isles farther south. When crossing the open sea Vikings sailed non-stop and, in good conditions with a competent crew, 160–190 km could be covered in twenty-four hours.

The arrival of Viking ships on Irish soil was probably not surprising. North-eastern England was already affected and no doubt word had spread to Irish monks. Only two years after the initial attack on the island monastery of Lindisfarne, the first recorded assault on Ireland, in 795, was short and brutal, being described in the *Annals of Ulster* as 'the burning of Rechru [the church and its shrine on Rathlin Island, Co. Antrim] by the

Toy boat from Christchurch Place, Dublin. The hole towards the left is where the steering board was attached, while the hole in the prow may reflect the common practice of towing a smaller vessel containing provisions behind the main ship on long voyages.

33

Above: Aerial view of the ruins at Clonmacnoise on the River Shannon. In 936 Dublin-based Vikings spent a two-night stopover stripping the monastery of movable wealth. Clonmacnoise may have been seen to be under the control of rival Vikings in Limerick.

Below: Irish or Scottish reliquary (container for holy relics), now in Copenhagen, bearing the runic inscription 'Rannveig owns this casket'. It may have been looted to serve as a woman's trinket box before being returned to its original use as a shrine.

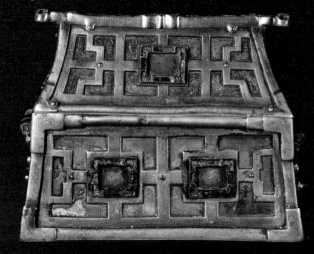

heathens'. Three years later it was the turn of Inis Pátraic, just offshore from Skerries in Co. Dublin, after which the Vikings took cattle tribute (tax) from surrounding territories, broke shrines and made 'great incursions' in Ireland and Scotland.

The fear and dread of a monastic community survives in written form, squeezed into the margins of a manuscript compiled in Co. Down. An Irish scribe was compelled to write this short poem:

> The wind is rough tonight
> Tossing the white-combed ocean
> I need not dread fierce Vikings
> Crossing the Irish sea

More threateningly, ships packed with Viking armies began to attack and control parts of coastal Ireland as early as the 830s. In 837 a fleet of sixty ships appeared on the Boyne and later the same year another fleet on the Liffey, their crews plundering 'churches, forts and dwellings', as recorded in the *Annals of Ulster*.

Raids were always smash-and-grab, spontaneous opportunities but were often politically motivated. At least two-thirds of raids in the late ninth century have been linked to relationships between Irish dynasts and the Vikings. By then the former were staging alliances with Vikings to improve their own status. The Irish, however, were slow to harness the power of ships, preferring to attack and destroy individual

34

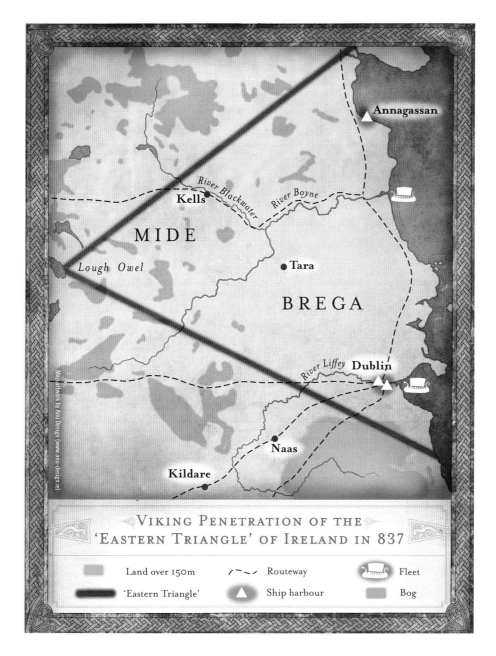

MIDE

BREGA

Annagassan

River Blackwater

River Boyne

Kells

Lough Owel

Tara

River Liffey Dublin

Naas

Kildare

Map artwork by Anú Design (www.anu-design.ie)

VIKING PENETRATION OF THE 'EASTERN TRIANGLE' OF IRELAND IN 837

▨	Land over 150m	⟋ ⌐ ⌐ ⟍	Routeway	⛴	Fleet
▬	'Eastern Triangle'	▲	Ship harbour	▨	Bog

Viking penetration of the 'eastern triangle' of Ireland in 837. By that date Viking raiders had a clear understanding of the strategic importance of this part of the island, it being the focal point of the five named highways (Irish *slighte*).

ships. In 921, under the leadership of the Northern Uí Néill king, Fergal, an Irish party wrecked a Viking vessel, killed the crew and took its bounty. It was not until the later Hiberno-Norse period, when Irish dynasts took over established towns, that they made use of the foreigners' fleets, as at Dublin and Limerick, to control Ireland's waterways and trade routes for themselves.

The Death of a Ship

A ship's journey did not always end when it was deemed no longer seaworthy. Ships played a part in pagan beliefs and myths, wherein they transported the dead to the afterworld. Found in Scandinavia, the Scottish Isles and the Isle of Man, ship burials can contain the remains of well-equipped high-status individuals, sometimes accompanied by food, slain horses and even servants. Usually an earthen mound was erected over the entire ship and its contents. Where ships were not affordable or available for burials, stones were arranged in the shape of a ship above ground to mark the burial area, as at Lindholm Høje in northern Jutland in Denmark. Elsewhere, to judge from literary evidence, ships were set alight and sent on a final voyage to sea with the remains of important individuals.

Above: Illustration of a small boat burial on the island of Sanday in the Orkneys. It contained the remains of a high-status woman and her slave. Sea-going vessels would have been all the more prized as sacrificial objects in such a treeless environment.

Right: Part of the great cemetery at Lindholm Høje. Although Jutland is short of durable stone, boat-shaped settings were a more economical memorial to the dead than ship burials. Alternatively circles, squares and triangles of upright stones would surround cremation sites.

FINDS BOX

A Viking Shipwreck

As many as 1,462 nautical miles from Dublin in the fjord bed of Roskilde harbour, Denmark, archaeologists made an incredible discovery connecting Dublin with the wider Viking world. Five shipwrecks were found and excavated in the 1960s, ranging from a small fishing boat to a large trading vessel and a warship. All had been deliberately scuttled to block two of three navigable channels through the area, preventing access to all but one route. The wreck known as Skuldelev 2 was the largest Viking warship ever discovered by that time and oak for building it was shown, through the use of dendrochronology, to have originated in forests in the Dublin region and been felled in 1042.

An ambitious experiment to understand better how Scandinavians built and sailed their ships was undertaken by the Viking Ship Museum in Roskilde in 2004. The experiment involved recreating the warship Skuldelev 2 using Viking Age tools and techniques. Built as a genuine reconstruction of a longship, it could carry sixty to 100 people. The experiment was a fascinating source of new information about the speed and navigability of ships and conditions on board. Under oars and with a moderate swell, a longship could reach a maximum speed of 4.2 knots. With a full wind, speeds of 13–17 knots were achieved.

The crew of this experimental vessel, known as *The Sea Stallion from Glendalough*, were divided into six sections, each with a foreman. In a longship, commands were shouted from one end of the vessel via an intermediary stationed in the middle. With a full crew, oar strokes were shorter for use in harbours or when the wind was absent or blowing in the wrong direction. The experiment also demonstrated that the crew had to work as a team and that, in such claustrophobic conditions, social skills were deemed just as important as the ability to sail.

The shipwreck Skuldelev 2 under excavation. In order to make archaeological excavation possible, a coffer-dam was installed around the wreck. Only about one-quarter of the original vessel survived, including key features such as the entire keelson and the sternpost.

The replica ship *Havhingsten fra Glendalough* (*The Sea Stallion from Glendalough*). With a crew of sixty volunteers it travelled from Roskilde, via choppy Scottish waters, to Dublin in 2007. The crew's experiences added to our understanding of Viking maritime life.

3
Warriors and Raiders

During the first millennium AD every culture had its warriors; Vikings were a Scandinavian manifestation of a universal phenomenon.

Every male Viking was trained how to fight and use weapons from an early age, yet most Scandinavians did not raid or take part in warfare. Many of those who did were probably ordinary farmers looking for the chance to improve their situation with some captured loot. These initial forces that arrived in Ireland relied largely on the elements of speed and surprise. Vikings – Scandinavians with a warrior identity – made up only a small section of Scandinavian society as a whole, yet their impact on Ireland and its population was brutal and significant. Their leaders, ambitious chieftains from Norway and Denmark, boldly vied for sovereignty over Dublin, creating political upheaval nationally and internationally with the Scandinavian kingdom of Dublin at the centre. At the same time Dublin-based Vikings were in competition with others elsewhere in Ireland, especially those in Limerick and Waterford, while in northern England York was a particular source of involvement during the formative period of 867–954.

Warrior Culture

'Cattle die, kindred die, every man is mortal. But I know one thing that never dies, the glory of the great dead.' So says the author of the Old Norse poem *Hávamál*. In Scandinavia, ties of kinship controlled how communities worked and members supported each other through a set of traditional rules of behaviour. Similarly, warriors were part of a *lið*, a warrior band of free men sustaining higher-ranking kings and chieftains. These military groups, some with personally hired members, followed and supported their leader. Whether loyal soldiers or mere opportunists, they shared a common warrior identity; in saga language, they were 'the men of the glittering spears'.

The image of a single-minded warrior band, tied together with shared military values and group solidarity, appears in heroic praise poetry of the time and in the later sagas. The tales relay deeds of inspirational leaders, oozing glory, honour and courage. The stories were like a handbook for warriors, warning

Below left: A Viking head carved on the wagon buried with the Oseberg ship. Representations of Vikings, in accordance with contemporary fashion, always feature a moustache and a beard. Life at sea and on campaign would have made regular shaving impracticable.

Below right: A selection of figures from chessmen found on the island of Lewis in the Outer Hebrides. The third swordsman from the left lacks a protective helmet and is biting the top of his shield, a supposed attribute of *berserkir*.

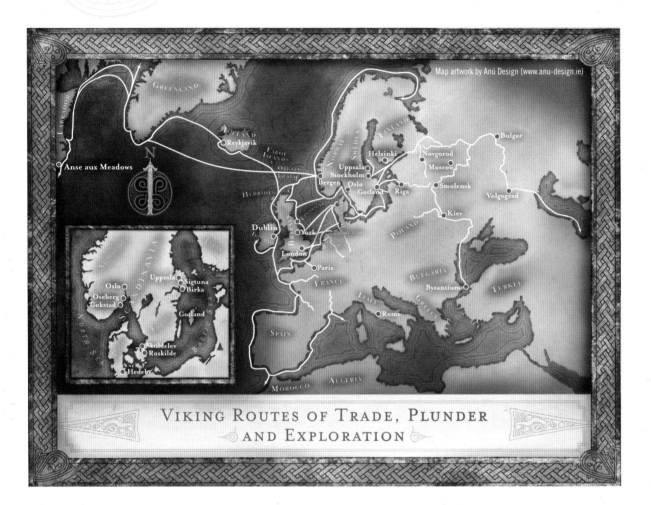

Map artwork by Anú Design (www.anu-design.ie)

VIKING ROUTES OF TRADE, PLUNDER AND EXPLORATION

Viking routes of trade, plunder and exploration. Without mastery of ship-building and navigation, the entire Viking phenomenon would not have occurred. There are other historical examples, such as Gothic architecture, where a particular field outstripped the prevailing level of technology.

against fleeing comrades on the battlefield and flattering brave leaders rewarded with well-gained booty. The actual horror of military duty is muted in the stories by the potential opportunity for glory. The eleventh-century author of the Irish *Fragmentary Annals* was more realistic: 'The shrieking of the javelins, and the crashing blows of swords, and the hammering of shields being struck, and the cries of soldiers being overcome, were loudly audible.'

There was no warrior caste as such, though the Viking world produced many war-bands. The mainly fictional *Jómsvikinga Saga* tells of a disciplined force of warriors recruited from men aged between eighteen and fifty. Their military code included sharing the spoils, absences for not longer than three days, and a total ban on contact with women. On the latter point, we know that by the 890s Danes operating in England had womenfolk as camp followers, but the Great Army had earlier shown remarkable discipline. A peculiarly Viking contribution

Dublin and the Viking World

to medieval militarism may have been the *berserkr*, 'bear-shirt'. In the later literature he appears as a frenzied fighter dressed in a distinctive garb, perhaps as part of ceremonial battle preparation, and it is a striking fact that this Old Norse word has entered the English language as 'berserk'.

That military activity shaded off into economic activity was characteristic of the Viking Age: warfare was as often as not a form of economic intercourse. Behind the aggression, brutality and destructiveness there was, as is commonly the case, calculating rationality. In effect Vikings were competing among themselves, and with the local inhabitants of the countries in which they raided, traded and settled, for wealth. Food and drink, bullion and cash, land and labour were among the considerable profits of Viking warfare. Even the womenfolk back home may have played a direct part: some of the loot found in western Norway in particular included items of reworked jewellery.

The Alfred Jewel found in Somerset in 1693. It belonged to King Alfred, that heroic and resourceful defender of his kingdom against Viking attacks. He was remarkable in many ways, including his ability to read his native Old English and translate from Latin.

A warrior culture was not unique to Viking society. Towards the end of the Viking Age, in the eleventh century, the sociological construct of the three orders of society was firmly established in parts of continental Europe. There were those who pray (the clergy), those who fight (the warriors) and those who work (the peasantry). This social theory was first articulated in the early Viking Age by King Alfred of Wessex, who in his translation of Boethius's *Consolation of Philosophy*, reflecting on the resources and tools needed by a king, observed that 'he must have praying men, fighting men and working men'. And as the Viking Age was drawing to a close in 1095, Pope Urban II encouraged Christian warriors to externalise their distinctive role in society by embarking on a crusade to Jerusalem.

Armies, Raiding Parties and Fleets

The size of Viking forces of every kind has been much debated. Partly this is because we have only their opponents' word for it: as the saying goes, the first casualty of warfare is the truth. Kings presumably commanded larger forces than chieftains, while some of the Danish armies seeking to conquer England in the late Viking Age were of a quite different order from Norwegian raiding parties

Maps showing campaigns in England by the Danish Great Army. Vikings had a much greater impact on England than on anywhere else in western Europe, destroying three of four kingdoms and leaving only Wessex in the south to fight again.

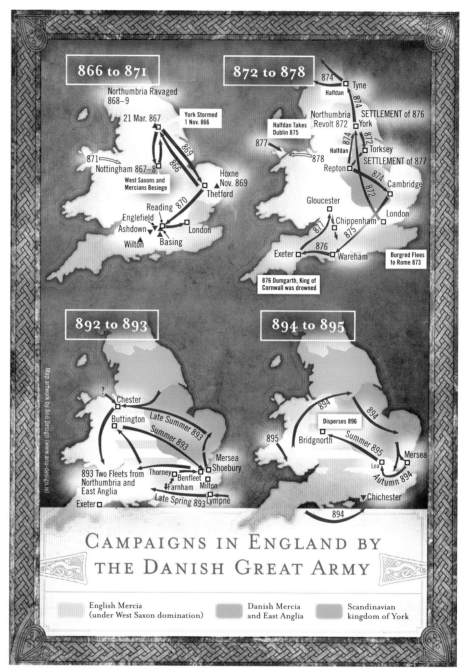

Map artwork by Anu Design (www.anu-design.ie)

866 to 871

Northumbria Ravaged 868–9
21 Mar. 867
York Stormed 1 Nov. 866
871
Nottingham 867–8
869
866
West Saxons and Mercians Besiege
Hoxne Nov. 869
Thetford
Reading 870
Englefield
Ashdown
Wilton
Basing
London

872 to 878

874 Tyne
Halfdan
874
874
Northumbria Revolt 872
SETTLEMENT of 876
York
Halfdan Takes Dublin 875
877
874
872
Halfdan
Torksey
878
SETTLEMENT of 877
Repton
874
872
Cambridge
Gloucester
877
Chippenham 875
London
Exeter 876 Wareham
Burgred Flees to Rome 873
876 Dumgarth, King of Cornwall was drowned

892 to 893

? Chester
Buttington
Late Summer 893
Summer 893
Mersea
Shoebury
893 Two Fleets from Northumbria and East Anglia
Thorney Benfleet
Farnham Milton
Late Spring 893 Lympne
Exeter

894 to 895

894
894
Disperses 896
895 Bridgnorth
Summer 895
Mersea
Lea
Autumn 894
894
Chichester
894

CAMPAIGNS IN ENGLAND BY THE DANISH GREAT ARMY

English Mercia (under West Saxon domination)   Danish Mercia and East Anglia   Scandinavian kingdom of York

in the early Viking Age. The dramatic successes of Sveinn Haraldsson (1013) and his son Knútr (1016) show that kingship in Denmark had been consolidated and made much more effective.

It is wise to adopt a cautious approach to the credibility of figures given in

annals and chronicles. As it happens, Irish annalists are notably restrained in their estimates of casualties on the enemy side: when in 837 the men of Brega, an Irish kingdom north of Dublin, 'routed' a plundering war-band, a total of 120 Vikings were reportedly killed. In 917, this time in Munster, only about a hundred men fell between the two sides, despite the stated fact that the fighting lasted for several hours. The main exception to this restraint comes in 848 when, in four battles in different parts of Ireland, between 240 and 1200 Viking dead are claimed in the annals. Contemporary Irish sources are somewhat less hostile in their reports than their English and continental counterparts, perhaps because it was relatively common for Irishmen to fight side by side with Scandinavian allies.

The most famous large-scale invasion force is the Danish Great Army that terrorised England and northern France in the period 865 to 896. Referred to in Old English as *micel here* and in Latin as *magnus exercitus*, both meaning 'great army', this was clearly regarded by contemporaries as being out of the ordinary. Led by several kings and numerous jarls, it did not arrive all at once but at intervals and in different locations, starting in eastern England. Having failed to overcome Alfred the Great's West Saxons, the Great Army crossed over to France in 879 but was unsuccessful again in the dramatic and drawn-out siege of Paris in 885–6. It returned to England in 892, failed to make inroads there and finally dispersed at Bridgnorth on the River Severn.

Viking attacks of all kinds were heavily dependent for their success on Scandinavian mastery of ship-building and navigation. The size of Viking fleets has also been a matter of scholarly debate. Contemporary written records offer two types of figure. One is small, precise, and usually associated with circumstantial details. Thus a mere six crews inflicted severe damage on the Isle of Wight in the year of the Great Army's dispersal, while seven shiploads of warriors ravaged Southampton and killed or captured most of its inhabitants nearly a century later. The other type of figure is much bigger and normally a round number, suggestive of an estimate. The more conservative of these figures are credible enough.

Artist's impression of a typical Viking raid. Irrespective of numbers in an 'army', a single ship's crew could create devastation among undefended civilians. Note the round tower in the distance and use of the horse as a weapon of warfare.

Left: Frankish image of a fully manned Viking ship from *c.* 1100. By then chainmail armour and kite-shaped shields were more typical of Christian knights, but the principal weapon is still the sturdy thrusting spear. Note the steersman incorrectly positioned on the right rather than the left.

Right: Ship and crewmen depicted on the Tjängvide picture-stone, Gotland. The eighth-century image shows how well established was the use of ocean-going warships before the conventional beginning of the Viking Age. Again note the steersman on the right.

Armies campaigning among hostile populations depended on their ships as a means of escape from their opponents as well as arrival. On big continental waterways the progress of a Viking fleet could serve as an advance warning to the local people, as in 853 when relics and other treasured possessions were removed to safety from Tours on the great River Loire in France. Farther away from the main rivers the presence of Vikings may have been unheralded: six years later the townspeople of Noyon were subjected to a night-time attack by Vikings based on the Seine, at least 85 km to the south-west, and the bishop and other noblemen were taken captive.

Weaponry and Defensive Armour

The stereotypical image of Viking warriors often paints an inaccurate picture. Heavy chainmail, shiny iron helmets, elaborate swords, spears and axes are regularly depicted as part of the usual Viking kit. In reality, warriors mostly wore their everyday clothes into battle with perhaps a padded tunic, fabricated like a thick duvet, and a pointed helmet of hardened leather for added protection. Ordinary warriors trained and fought without a sword, relying on spears, axes, bows and arrows, and shields. Helmets and mail shirts are extremely rare finds in furnished graves.

Dublin and the Viking World

Kings, chieftains and other wealthy warriors could afford swords. These precious items are frequently found in furnished graves, buried with the owner as a symbol of manhood and social status and a reflection of rank both in this life and in the next. Old swords were considered superior because they were thought to have been blood-hardened and to possess magical powers. Proud owners gave their swords names, such as Leg Biter or Viper. Some of these superior weapons are inscribed with the name Ulfberht, presumably a highly skilled craftsman working probably in the Rhineland.

Artist's impression of a Dublin warrior of the early Viking Age. Dublin's warrior community may have had a group identity expressed through their unique weaponry, including painted shield imagery, making them distinguishable on the battlefield from their Norse contemporaries.

Whereas Viking swords seem not to have been made in Ireland, other types of weapon were probably being produced locally. Examples can be seen in the National Museum of Ireland and are evidence of the new military technology that arrived on the Irish battlescape. Projectile spears, the commonest weapon

Petersen Type	No. of swords				
	Kilmainham–Islandbridge	Rest of Dublin	Rest of Ireland	Unprovenanced	Total (Ireland)
C	7	—	—	—	7
D	2	1	—	—	3
E	2	1	—	1	4
F	2	—	—	—	2
H	14	6	2	3	25
I	2	—	—	—	2
K	1	—	2	—	3
Type K variants, including Særtype 8	7	2	—	—	9
N	—	—	1	—	1
X	1	1	1	1	4
Unclassified	4	4	2	—	10
Total	42	15	8	5	70

Table of sword types from Irish Viking graves. The typology developed by the Swedish scholar Jan Petersen, published in 1919, is still used universally. The predominance of finds from Dublin, and especially Kilmainham and Islandbridge, is abundantly clear.

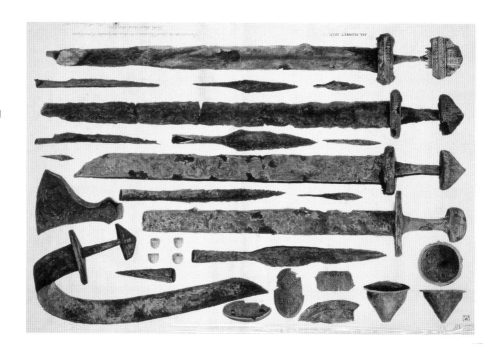

Watercolour by James Plunket of Viking Age grave-goods from railway cuttings at Kilmainham found in 1845. This is one of twelve paintings commissioned by the Royal Irish Academy at that time and presented to the Royal Society of Northern Antiquities, Copenhagen, two years later.

found in Irish Viking graves, and the battleaxe (previously unknown in Ireland) are types unlike those seen in pre-Viking contexts. The bow and projectile arrowheads had not been used in Ireland for centuries, but reappeared with the Vikings as a military rather than a hunting weapon.

The distinctive Dublin weapons are an amalgamation of types unseen anywhere else in the Viking world. During the ninth century the invaders produced shield bosses (and therefore shields) that were smaller than Scandinavian types and comparable to Irish and Anglo-Saxon styles. Similarly, small throwing spears were almost certainly derived from a local Irish prototype. They presented a contrast to the heavier thrusting spear for fighting at close quarters, whose socket was often decorated with grooves inlaid with silver, copper or brass, or some combination of these, creating a glittering effect.

Spearheads from Sastamala, Tampere and Turku in Finland. Decorated in the late Viking Age Urnes style, this type is found throughout the Nordic countries. Over a hundred have come from Finland and one-third of these are silver-plated and decorated.

Generally speaking, the furnished graves reflect the burial customs of Viking culture. Their contents may point to a conscious expression of kin-group identity, as families vied and died for power in the ninth and tenth centuries. Oaths were sworn on a leader's sword: such a weapon, recorded as the sword

of Carlus, was kept in Dublin and is last heard of in 1029 as part of the ransom demanded for the release of a son of King Sigtryggr Silkenbeard.

Warfare in the Viking Age was heavily dependent on loyalty. Of this we get a strong hint in the Welshman Asser's *Life of King Alfred*: referring to the battle of Ashdown (in Berkshire) in the winter of 870–1, he portrays 'one side [the Danes] acting wrongfully and the other side [the West Saxons] set to fight for life, loved ones and country'.

Military Tactics

Warfare on land consisted of pitched battles, skirmishes, duels and attacks by Viking bands on civilians. Pitched battles were rare since Vikings were vulnerable in the open countryside, even though horses were commonly available. When a pitched battle did occur, it is likely that the Vikings employed a compact linear formation, as commonly used by other peoples elsewhere in Europe since Roman times. Battle-lines might take the form of a central body of elite warriors and more mobile flanking wings on either side. Hostilities would have been initiated with a shower of light missiles – arrows, javelins and even stones – to test the opposition. Hand-to-hand combat would then follow in a series of skirmishes between two groups. The ultimate aim was to force the opposing army to give ground first, break ranks and flee.

Despite their reputed military prowess, Vikings were not supermen. In Ireland at least, they killed and were killed in unequal proportions. In the period 917–1014, following on from their recapture of Dublin, about twenty-five military engagements took place between Irish armies and Viking forces from Dublin,

Re-enactors practising fighting with spears. In sagas many men are killed by a spear thrust rather than a sword slash. In some, possibly exaggerated cases, the victim is hoisted into the air on a spear before being cast down again.

Artist's impression of the large-scale pitched battle fought in 937 at an unknown location in England named Brunanburh. The victors were West Saxons led by King Æthelstan; the losers were Dublin-based Vikings led by King Óláfr Góðfriðsson, who nevertheless survived.

the latter sometimes containing Irish allies. Of these, the purely Irish forces won fifteen, most notably the battle of Tara in 980. In hand-to-hand fighting at close quarters, Irish superior strength in numbers would give an advantage as one battle-line or the other gave way and fell back.

Tactics used by Vikings were similar to those used by native forces. A standard ploy was to threaten destructive violence with a view to exacting tribute. Vikings engaged in this process in the west Frankish kingdom in 866 had come equipped not only with weapons, but also with their own balance scales for weighing the 4000 pounds of silver they demanded. Another tactic was to target large gatherings of people. In 929 Dublin Vikings scheduled a raid on St Brigit's shrine at Kildare on her feast day, when pilgrims gathered together formed a crowd of potential hostages and slaves. The burning of religious shrines was also a way of forcing compliance from the Irish, as was the exaction of cattle tribute. Taking valuable livestock ensured protection money, collateral and, at the very least, food. Cattle raiding, of course, was nothing new in Ireland.

Vikings made extensive use of defensive enclosures. Strongholds became necessary when raiders were attempting to establish themselves among hostile populations in England, Frankia (modern France) and Ireland. For their conquest of parts of England after 865, the Danes built a series of winter camps. These were temporary yet effective bases, often sited on a natural island or on a neck of land where a side-stream met the main river. (At Dublin, both possibilities for camp bases existed.) An archaeologically attested example is at Repton in England's Trent valley, where a D-shaped enclosure is believed to represent the documented winter camp of 873–4, whose establishment presaged the collapse of the kingdom of Mercia in central England.

There was no distinctively Viking method of warfare; the Scandinavians adapted to circumstances. As well as their social structure and legal customs,

Dublin and the Viking World

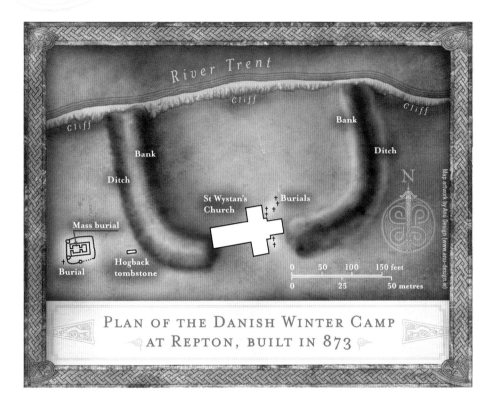

PLAN OF THE DANISH WINTER CAMP
AT REPTON, BUILT IN 873

River Trent

cliff   cliff   cliff

Bank

Bank   Ditch

Ditch

St Wystan's   ✝ Burials
Church   ✝
✝
Mass burial   ✝

N

✝
Burial   Hogback   0   50   100   150 feet
tombstone   0   25   50 metres

Map artwork by Anu Design (www.anu-design.ie)

Left: Plan of the Danish winter camp at Repton, built in 873. Use was made of the existing church, most Viking burials being outside the enclosure. *Longphuirt* in Ireland were often designed along similar lines, access by river being essential.

Below: Artist's impression of one of five administrative and tax-gathering centres from the time of Haraldr Bluetooth, king of Denmark, c. 980. By then Denmark was by far the most advanced of the Viking homelands and poised for a conquest of England.

they had for the most part inherited a shared northern European tradition of war-making. 'Free' men were distinguished partly by freedom to carry weapons, and thus *all* free men might be capable of fighting. Farmers and traders needed to be able to protect themselves in a society without a police force. In a world lacking bank vaults all movable wealth was vulnerable. Effective kingship and effective lordship would modify these conditions only gradually.

FINDS BOX

Warrior Burials

In 2003 Linzi Simpson and a team of archaeologists excavating in Dublin's city centre uncovered the remains of four Viking skeletons. It is thought that these Vikings were part of an elite warrior force active in Dublin in the early ninth century and possibly residents of the recorded *longphort* (ship harbour). Two of these warriors were found to be Scandinavian and two were from the Scottish isles.

One of these skeletons and the objects buried with him revealed some startling information. He was a strong, robust individual, tall at 1.76 m. His bones indicated that he was between seventeen and twenty-five years old when he died. His spine showed signs of schmorl's nodes – wear on the bone as a result of physical hardship in childhood. He was right-handed and marks on his shoulders indicate that he was well practised in the rotation movement needed to swing a weapon. The remains were disturbed after burial and it is likely that a shield and sword were extracted by a grave-robber.

Remains of a warrior discovered on South Great George's Street, Dublin. The warrior was native to Norway and metal shards discovered around his remains suggest that he practised metal smithing. A smith was an invaluable addition to a raiding party.

Right: A comb made from antler discovered in the same warrior's grave. The teeth of the comb were crafted close together, making it ideal for ridding hair of lice and dirt. Viking material culture shows a keen awareness of personal hygiene.

4
Traders and Settlers

Vikings as sea-pirates engaged in raiding,
but some of them and their descendants turned
to trading and settling

Raiding, trading and settling were distinct activities, yet they could coincide in the Viking Age. The basic necessities for human survival – food and drink, clothing and shelter – were equally essential for piratical raiders. While non-perishable items such as clothes and tents could be transported on board ships, fresh food and drink had to be sourced on arrival. Interaction with the peoples of western Europe, including Ireland, would have been normal from the start of the Viking Age.

Round tower at Clondalkin serving primarily as a belfry regulating religious life. Plundered by Vikings in 833, this monastery appears nevertheless to have survived, despite being situated only 6.5 km west of the pagan Kilmainham and Islandbridge burial complex.

Relations were sometimes peaceful and sometimes violent, depending on local circumstances and other variables such as the season of the year. Eventually, in certain districts, the combination of raiding and trading activity led to settlement. Part of northern France became known as Normandy, the land of the Northmen. Settlement could take different forms: temporary or permanent, rural or urban, political or non-political. Viking Age Dublin and its immediate hinterland demonstrate all of these settlement forms. Along with York in northern England, Dublin has one of the most informative archaeological and historical records of the western colonies.

The Silver Economy

Almost any commodity or object can be used as currency, provided that there is broad agreement as to its value. Examples from elsewhere in medieval Europe of commodities used in this way include butter in Norway, calves in Hungary, fur in Russia and linen in Bohemia. Farther afield, we hear of currencies in cocoa beans in Mexico, grain in India, salt in China and whales' teeth in Fiji.

Pre-Viking, early medieval Ireland started with a dual currency. The prime

Selection from the Sejrø hoard, Denmark. Silver could circulate in various forms for trading: ingots, hacksilver, ring money, coins and jewellery. The biggest hoards, including the one found by chance at Cuerdale in north-western England, contain an impressive mixture.

Map showing exports and imports around the Viking world. Supplies of silver came from western Asia, mainly via Birka in central Sweden, into northern Europe before *c.* 975. Dublin became a vital and wealthy link in North Atlantic trading.

economic resource was cows, which were used both for actual payments and for estimating amounts in other goods. The most famous individual who dealt in cows as currency was Brian Bórama (Brian Boru) – his name means 'the tribute-taker in cows'. Cattle continued to function as a currency unit for many more centuries in Gaelic Ireland. The other key commodity was female slaves; according to a well-known text, one of these equalled in value three milch cows.

On occasion precious metals – gold and silver – were used for specific payments, but they were in short supply at the start of the Viking Age in Ireland. Vikings made a difference to this in two ways, one of which was the obvious method of 'dishoarding' many ecclesiastical treasuries of their decorated metalwork. On the other hand, they increased the supply of bullion, particularly silver, into Ireland. Viking Age silver circulated in the form of bars or ingots as well as jewellery and ornaments.

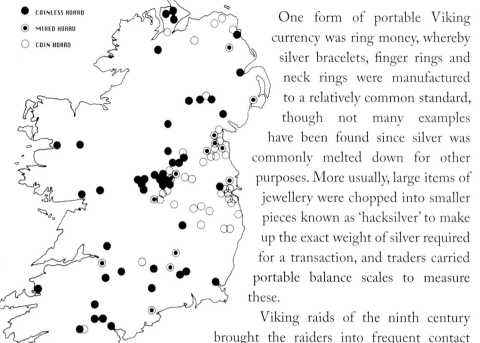

Map showing the distribution of silver hoards of the early Viking Age in Ireland. Notice the big concentration of coinless hoards in the Westmeath area and the large number of coin hoards found in other Irish territories distributed around Dublin.

● COINLESS HOARD
◉ MIXED HOARD
○ COIN HOARD

One form of portable Viking currency was ring money, whereby silver bracelets, finger rings and neck rings were manufactured to a relatively common standard, though not many examples have been found since silver was commonly melted down for other purposes. More usually, large items of jewellery were chopped into smaller pieces known as 'hacksilver' to make up the exact weight of silver required for a transaction, and traders carried portable balance scales to measure these.

Viking raids of the ninth century brought the raiders into frequent contact with the Frankish empire, which had a strong centralised coinage introduced by Charlemagne. During the tenth century silver became more plentiful in the Viking homelands, thanks to the massive influx of Kufic coins from the Near East. More than 85,000 Arabic coins dating from the ninth and tenth centuries have been found in Scandinavia. Scandinavian traders thus became accustomed to dealing with coinage and some rulers began to issue their own coins.

In the late ninth and early tenth centuries the majority of the silver in Ireland took the form of whole ornaments, ingots or hacksilver. By the mid-tenth century there had been fundamental changes in the use of silver with the emergence in some areas of a mixed coin and hacksilver 'dual economy'. Dublin and some inland areas became increasingly accustomed to the use of imported Anglo-Saxon coins. Coin hoards found in a semicircular swathe of territory around Dublin suggest that the Irish were adopting the practice of using coins, if only on a small scale.

Towards the end of the period, this use culminated in the minting of coins. In the mid-990s Sigtryggr Silkenbeard, one of the most successful of Dublin's Hiberno-Norse rulers, had Ireland's first coins struck. His decision represents an important shift in the monetary history of the town and the beginning of a 'national' currency in Ireland. His coins were closely modelled on Anglo-Saxon prototypes.

The Slave Trade

Until the middle of the tenth century the wealth of Viking Dublin was based on one major commodity – slaves. When Vikings raided a settlement, they took away not only treasure and supplies but also people. Some were ransomed or put to work on the Vikings' own farms, but the majority were shipped to slave markets to be traded for silver or other goods. Some of these slave markets were located in Spain or even as far away as southern Russia. Men, women and children were kidnapped from all over Europe; defeat in warfare was another major source of supply.

Vikings did not have a monopoly on slaving; it was widespread throughout the known world. Vikings themselves were sometimes captured and sold into slavery, which was the fate that befell many of them after Dublin was attacked by the Irish in 944. Stories about slaves are recorded, including a nun (who sang psalms to prove who she was) rescued from slavery by Rimbert in Denmark in exchange for his horse and its gear, according to the Life of this minor saint.

Below: Reconstruction of a Dublin Type 2 house. This smaller house type tended to stand behind the larger Type 1 main dwelling. Floor areas were more completely covered in wattle mats, suggesting use as sleeping quarters, perhaps for slaves.

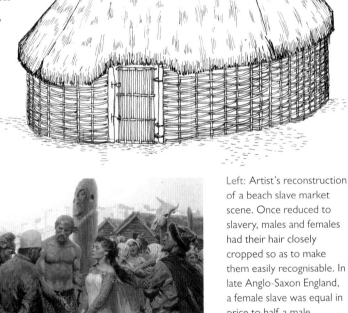

Left: Artist's reconstruction of a beach slave market scene. Once reduced to slavery, males and females had their hair closely cropped so as to make them easily recognisable. In late Anglo-Saxon England, a female slave was equal in price to half a male.

VIKING AGE SETTLEMENT IN ICELAND

Land above 500 metres

Area of tephra deposit
from Mt Hekla, 1104

• Excavated settlement

Area of place-names
from Landnámabók

Ice cap

Pagan grave

Across most of Europe a legal distinction between free men and women, on the one hand, and unfree men and women, on the other hand, was more or less universal. Servitude of various kinds is found in Celtic, Germanic (including Scandinavian) and Slavic societies. The most obvious and abject form of unfreedom was chattel slavery. The word 'chattel' is equivalent to 'cattle'; human beings were owned by other human beings. Slaves belonged in principle to a master or mistress from birth until death and the condition of slavery was inherited by any children born of slaves. Their market value could be quite low, with the result that even ordinary farmers might own two or three slaves for agrarian and domestic work.

A great deal of Viking raiding and trading may have been concerned with slaves and slave markets, sometimes resulting in enforced emigration to countries and cultures that were totally unfamiliar. Language was an immediate problem for many slaves. A feature of the Gulathing Law transmitted to Iceland from Norway was that lighter punishments for certain offences were prescribed for foreign-born slaves. In Ireland there was a ready-made domestic demand for slaves. Opportunities for exporting slaves arose in the 870s onwards, as Iceland was opened up for settlement. Men were needed to clear the land, to haul timber and turf, and to manage domestic animals; women, both free-born and servile, were required for all manner of domestic duties. About fourteen percent of the recorded settlers in Iceland had Celtic associations, to judge by their names, while Celtic slaves and concubines were probably numerous in the new colony.

Genetic evidence can be mined for information about Viking slavery. The Y-chromosome is passed on from father to son like a surname and is good for distinguishing the origin of male populations. Recent studies suggest that over twenty percent of Icelandic founding males had Gaelic ancestry, with the remainder having Norse ancestry. These findings accord with studies of mitochondrial DNA in Icelandic women, which is passed on only from mother to daughter, giving a picture of female lineages. Mitochondrial work has shown that about half of Iceland's founding females were of Gaelic ancestry. Many of these men and women are likely to have been slaves.

Dublin may well have been the biggest slave market in Britain and Ireland. The most dramatic indicator comes in 871 when Dublin's joint kings returned from Scotland with an estimated two hundred shiploads of English, British and Pictish prisoners. Vikings may have learnt to time their raids to coincide with

Opposite page: Early settlement in Iceland according to *Landnámabók*, the 'Book of Settlements'. The first two generations of settlers were mostly concentrated in the south-western and western coastal margins of this volcanic island and along the main river valleys of the north.

Dalkey Island viewed from Coliemore Harbour. Large numbers of captives were held on this island, one of whom was an abbot who was drowned as he tried to escape in 939.

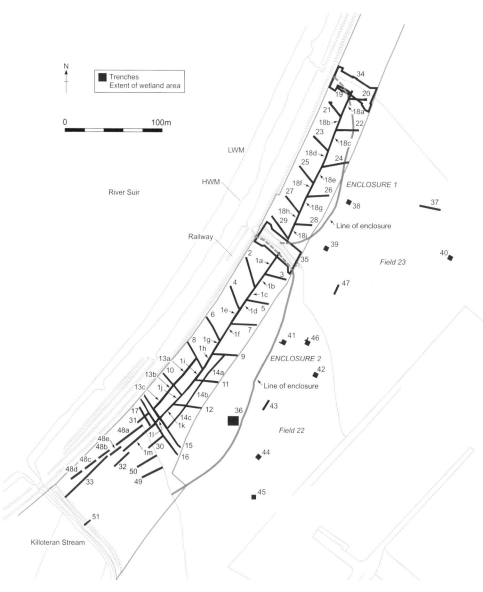

Trenches
Extent of wetland area

0   100m

LWM

River Suir

HWM

Railway

34
19   20
21   18a
18b   22
23   18c
18d   24
25   18e
18f   26   ENCLOSURE 1
27   38
18h   18g   37
29   28   Line of enclosure
18i
2   35   39
1a   40
3   Field 23
4   1b   47
1c
1e   1d   5
6   1f   7   41   46
8   1g   9   ENCLOSURE 2
1h   42
13a   1i   Line of enclosure
13b   10   14a
13c   1j   11   43
17   14b   Field 22
31   12   36
48a   14c
48e   1l   1k
48b   30   15
1m   16
48c   32   50
48d   33   49
51

Killoteran Stream

Right: Plan of the enclosure site at Woodstown, Co. Waterford. Industrial activity, especially metalworking, was combined with trading in this ninth-century Viking riverside settlement in Ireland. Like the first recorded Viking settlement at Dublin, it may be understood as a *longphort*, 'ship harbour'.

Below: Balance scales, pan and chains found at Islandbridge in Dublin, which can be associated with six decorated weights. Vikings are known to have brought their own equipment with them on plundering expeditions, both for the division of loot and for peaceful trading.

major religious festivals, perhaps with the aid of their Christian womenfolk. When King Máel Sechnaill II of Mide (Meath) captured Dublin in 981, he is said to have freed large numbers of hostages from all over the country.

The Dublin Emporium

Before the reign of Óláfr Kvaran (945–80) Dublin is probably best thought of as a trading settlement or emporium, rather than a regular town. There was a distinct air of impermanence about early Viking Dublin, with a period of enforced exile by an Irish coalition, at least for the socio-political elite, from 902 to 917, followed by attempts by a succession of rulers to take over the kingship of

A selection of decorated weights from Islandbridge. Fragments of high-quality decorated metalwork representative of the eighth-century Irish style were adapted for use as weights by Vikings. At least some of the warriors of Viking Dublin were engaged in trading activity.

York. Two other trading settlements, Annagassan in Co. Louth and Woodstown in Co. Waterford, appear to have been relatively short-lived enterprises.

Archaeology provides us with some clues as to the mechanics of trading. Many of the artefacts associated with trade in Ireland came from the Kilmainham and Islandbridge grave-field. Four relatively complete balance scales have been found in this location and a further sixty or so are known from other parts of Viking Age Europe. There is a notable concentration of scales in Norway's Vestfold district, probably a reflection of the importance of Kaupang as a trading settlement. The decoration on some of the Kilmainham and Islandbridge scales is directly comparable to that on Norwegian examples.

Several Viking weights were also recovered in the nineteenth century from the pagan grave fields at Kilmainham and Islandbridge, some of which are made of lead, capped with pieces of decorative metalwork. In addition to these antiquarian discoveries, a large number of smaller, generally undecorated lead weights have been recovered from archaeological excavations in Dublin's habitation deposits. The decorated weights appear to represent a unit of approximately 25–26 g, though the precise mathematical implications are still a matter of research.

The remains of two purses – comparatively rare survivals from the Viking world – were found at the Islandbridge grave field. These would have been attached to some organic material, probably thin leather or a piece of textile. Such purses may have been fitted on a belt worn around the waist. The size of both purses suggests

Purse mounts of copper alloy from Islandbridge. The U-shaped binding strips delineate the dimensions of the purse, while the pieces of sheet metal with a central slot may have served to attach the purse to a belt.

that they were intended to hold small, relatively valuable items such as hacksilver or weights. Some Vikings can be thought of as an early type of businessmen.

We have no idea of the number of permanent settlers in the Dublin emporium. In those parts of Europe that were settled by Vikings, the traditional way of indicating settlement density and distribution is to map place-names of Scandinavian or part-Scandinavian types. There are very few place-names of purely Scandinavian type anywhere in Ireland, including the Dublin region. Most of the names containing a Norse element are really of Irish origin, suggesting a mixed culture from the start. 'Viking' Dublin was never purely Viking.

Coinage and the Dublin Mint

Representing the fifth generation of Scandinavian kings of Dublin, Sigtryggr Silkenbeard (989–1036) inherited this mixed culture along with strong links to Anglo-Danish England. His father, Óláfr Kvaran, had in his own younger years attempted twice, unsuccessfully, to be accepted as the king of York, shortly before that kingdom's absorption into the West Saxon political sphere in 954. Early in his reign, in the mid-990s, Sigtryggr made his decisive gesture of modernisation by instituting a local coinage in Dublin, which was the first ever to be made in Ireland.

The Hiberno-Norse currency, as it is known, went through several phases; its history is complicated. The initial model was the penny of Æthelred II of England, whose kingdom was issuing large numbers of coins in an effort to pay periodic tribute (*danegeld*) to Danish Vikings. In fact, payment of tribute is a possible explanation for Sigtryggr's decision. In 997 Dublin, together with the rest of southern Ireland, acquired an ambitious new Irish overlord in the person of Brian Bórama. Silver pennies were much more portable than cows for Vikings travelling from Dublin to Brian's home territory at Kincora, near Killaloe in Co. Clare, to pay tribute to him.

The weight of the Dublin coins soon decreased, however, representing a currency devaluation against that of King Knútr's England. From the 1030s onwards the Dublin currency declined in other ways, both stylistically and in terms of the lettering of the inscriptions. By the end of the century there was

Dublin and the Viking World

MINTS IN ENGLAND 957–1016

- ■ Existing mints
- ● New mints of Edward the Martyr
- ◉ New mints of Æthelred II from 1000
- ▭ New mints of Edgar
- ◎ New mints of Æthelred II to 999

Map artwork by Anú Design (www.anu-design.ie)

Left: Reconstruction of a moneyer at work from the Dublinia exhibition. The names of the moneyer and of the place of mintage were placed on well-designed coins. We do not know where in Dublin the Hiberno-Norse coins were struck, but presumably near the royal compound.

Right: Contemporary manuscript image of King Knútr and his Norman wife Emma presenting an altar cross to the New Minster in Winchester. Sigtryggr of Dublin probably visited Knútr at his English court at least once before the latter's sudden death in 1035.

an array of styles and motifs, and the coins weighed less than forty percent of Sigtryggr's first issues. In the end, bracteates – thin copper discs – resembling trading tokens rather than proper coins were being struck. These bracteates may have been issued by the merchant elite for local exchanges, as was the case at that time elsewhere in northern Europe.

The fact of the matter is that coins were not deemed essential to trading. Dublin, under direct or indirect Irish control for the most part after 1052, was able to continue as a major economic power without the use of good-quality coins. A settled population of craftsmen and traders, clergy and laity must have been engaged in a bullion economy along with old-fashioned bartering for most purposes. There is nothing surprising here: nowadays vast amounts of trading, national and international, take place through the medium of electronic calculations and devices, while coins remain in favour to pay for a bus fare or a drink in the local pub.

FINDS BOX

The Dublin Silver Hoards

Prior to the excavations at Castle Street and Werburgh Street, Dublin had produced only one precious metal hoard, found *c.* 1870 during the restoration of Christ Church Cathedral. Three recently discovered hoards comprise nearly 450 coins in total. These hoards also bridge a gap that had formerly existed in the Irish hoard record of the late tenth century. Having been assembled beyond the tight regulation of coinage (Latin *renovatio monetae*) in England, the Dublin coin hoards can assist with the analysis of late Anglo-Saxon coinage.

Two of these hoards were uncovered during excavations in advance of construction work at Castle Street in 1993. The smaller and earlier hoard, known as Castle Street (1), contains seventy-nine coins, while Castle Street (2) is composed of 242 coins. A third hacksilver hoard comprising two silver torques and one of iron was also recovered from this site and is the only hoard of its type yet to have been discovered in Dublin. These coin hoards were located in an area of domestic occupation under a raised seating or bedding space. Some of the coins were found together in 'rolls', suggesting that they were being stored in this manner rather than loose in a bag or box.

The Werburgh Street hoard was discovered in a layer of organic material in a truncated building and may have been in a bag that had decomposed. This hoard of 125 coins was found at a level containing a number of houses known to archaeologists as Type 1 Dublin buildings (typical main residential houses) together with evidence of industrial metalworking.

The dating of the three hoards is fairly consistent. Castle Street (1) is the earliest, while the Castle Street (2) and Werburgh Street hoards are slightly later and strikingly similar in content. The hoards were probably deposited within a few years of each other between the late 980s and the mid-990s and represent the silver in use in Dublin immediately prior to King Sigtryggr's coinage.

Above: Six coins from the Castle Street (2) hoard, now on display in the National Museum of Ireland. The hoard consists of imported Anglo-Saxon coinage that appeared in Dublin during the tenth century, suggesting a fairly consistent and two-way relationship with England.

Above: Reverse of six coins from the Castle Street (2) hoard. Of the total of 242 coins discovered, forty-three mints were represented including Canterbury, London, Oxford and York. The kings named on the coins were Edgar, Edward the Martyr and Æthelred II.

5

Craft-workers

*Viking Age Scandinavia belonged to the late
Iron Age, at which time ironworking was supremely
important, but many other materials were also used
in this highly diversified culture*

In most cultures, practical traditions are preserved over the generations as men and women inherit and pass on a wide range of skills. Many of those skills involve crafting or making things. For late Iron Age Scandinavians in the Viking period, craftsmanship was a normal part of life in which most people made useful items for themselves. In addition to this, some people were specialists in a particular craft, to the extent that they could earn a living in that way. While craft activity could and did take place in a rural environment, the acquisition of raw materials and the prospect of making sales could be conducted more efficiently in a town. In this chapter the basic raw materials have been categorised into three main classes – botanical (plant-based), metal (including iron) and animal products. Examples of each will be given in turn; they tell a succession of stories of human ingenuity and resourcefulness.

Plants

In the Viking world, a good farm was one that harboured plentiful natural resources, including a variety of botanical ones. Large structures such as defensive palisades and gateways, houses and outbuildings, ships and boats required heavy timber from both broadleaved hardwoods and coniferous softwoods, whereas an extensive range of smaller items were crafted from lighter woods. Softer materials were used to insulate house walls and to cover their roofs; some of these could be gathered from the natural environment, while others, such as straw, were by-products of farming. In watery areas, reeds and rushes were valuable resources for basketwork.

The carpentry of early Viking Dublin has been described as conservative and simple. The roof structures of houses do not survive in the archaeological record and there is much uncertainty as to the arrangement of the main timbers and how they were fastened together. Evidence from entrance jambs, thresholds and bench frames suggests construction with minimum joinery. What are called notch and tenon or scarf joints were generally used. Squared ash beams for entrance posts were fashioned using axes and roughly finished. Grooves for

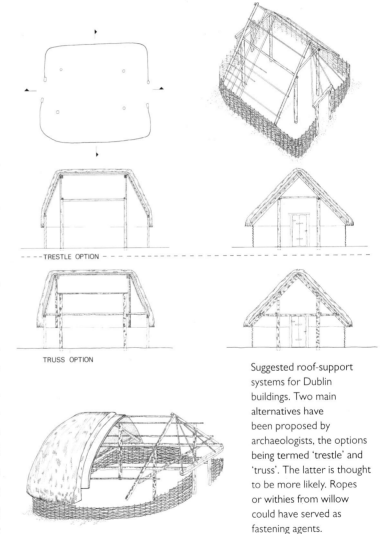

– – – TRESTLE OPTION – – – – – – – –

TRUSS OPTION

Suggested roof-support systems for Dublin buildings. Two main alternatives have been proposed by archaeologists, the options being termed 'trestle' and 'truss'. The latter is thought to be more likely. Ropes or withies from willow could have served as fastening agents.

Stave-built wooden bucket of Irish origin from the Oseberg ship burial, Vestfold in Norway, which contained the richly furnished graves of two women. The red and yellow geometric enamelled decoration is paralleled in the art of the Book of Durrow (Co. Offaly).

Conical keg from High Street, Dublin, tenth century. The central hole with a decorated swivelling lid was used to fill the vessel, a wooden tube acted as a spout and the paired perforations probably held a rope handle for lifting.

FINDS BOX

Coopers and Cooperage

The craft of cooperage involves the specialist manufacture and repair of stave-built vessels for household or commercial use. Cooperage was an established tradition in Ireland prior to the Viking Age, where yew was the preferred species. Wet coopering, that is, the production of casks for the storage and transportation of valuable liquids, probably arrived in Ireland around the middle of the first millennium AD.

Excavations around Wood Quay yielded 1,872 coopered components, mostly domestic tableware (drinking and serving vessels) and household items such as churns, kegs and buckets. These vessels were supplied both by coopers working in the town and also imported from elsewhere in Ireland and from overseas. Most of the coopered vessels from Viking-Age Dublin are open-topped, truncated cones measuring 100 mm to 300 mm in height. Only a few tops and bottoms of casks are represented, indicating that these were heavily reused.

The tenth-century assemblage is dominated by yew-wood vessels in the Irish tradition with yew staves and binding hoops, whereas oak is evident in larger vessels of the eleventh century. There is a peak in the use of softwoods (pine and spruce) in the mid-tenth to mid-eleventh centuries, reflecting strong contact with the Scandinavian homelands.

Although most of the surviving wood was plain and unadorned, the late Viking Age has also yielded decorated wooden objects of various kinds. Several examples of decorated boxes, crooks, knife handles, spatulas, strap ends and weavers' swords have been discovered. Others from Dublin are unique or at least rare: a human figurine, a pulley block (part of a lifting device), a saddlebow and a toy horse. Some of these wooden objects exhibit a fusion of Insular (that is, from Ireland and Britain) and Viking taste, whilst eleventh-century objects echo the slightly earlier Anglo-Saxon 'Winchester style', coinciding with the reign of Sigtryggr Silkenbeard in Dublin and that of Knútr the Great in England.

retaining horizontal wall wattles (thin interlaced branches and twigs) were made either by a combination of drilling a series of holes for the upright poles and then chiselling away between them or, as tools advanced, by chiselling in a sill beam (heavy foundation timber) to hold the ends of the wattle panels.

Dublin's waterlogged archaeological deposits have yielded an important body of evidence for the cooper's craft-working. A broad range of stave-built vessels (using shaped vertical staves bound with hoops) was being produced from the late tenth century onwards, much of it domestic tableware but also larger kegs and casks. The choice of yew as the dominant wood used has led to the interesting conclusion that most of Dublin's coopers were either Irishmen or working in an Irish tradition. Multicultural life was being led in Viking Dublin from early on.

Another material that belies its botanical nature is amber, the petrified resin of pine trees. Amber has been found in numerous archaeological contexts across northern Europe in its raw state, as part-finished objects and as sophisticated jewellery. Beads are the commonest amber product, but other finds include amulets, gaming pieces and pendants. Production could be on an industrial scale: a single house in Dublin's Fishamble Street yielded 136 complete beads and much more besides, its corner compartments being used both for craft-working and for storage. Amber was an exotic import not available in Ireland. Once worked into attractively coloured jewellery and polished, it was highly desirable and fashionable.

Wooden zoomorphic crook or handle and a figurine or gaming piece from Fishamble Street, Dublin, eleventh century. Several so-called crooks have been found in Dublin, but their purpose and symbolism – religious or secular – are uncertain.

Metals

In an Iron Age culture, the blacksmith was perhaps the most important craftsman, working mainly, though not exclusively, in iron (Old Norse *járn*). The two pairs of tongs recovered from furnished graves at Islandbridge may represent the social status of metalworking as much as their potential utility in an afterlife. Smiths made and repaired tools for other craftsmen, including agricultural and fishing implements, equestrian equipment such as bits and stirrups, keys for strong-boxes, rivets for ship-building, and weapons. There were a number of sources for iron ore and part of central Sweden in the Viking Age was called Jämtland, 'iron country'.

Iron was sometimes used along with other metals for small, refined objects such as pins, rings and tweezers. Items of copper alloy were made of hammered sheet

Amber pendants from Fishamble Street, Dublin. The commonest shape for pendants found in this part of the town was trapezoidal, perhaps with symbolic significance. The cruciform (cross-shaped) type may be indicative of Christian influence, which would have been ever-present in Viking Dublin.

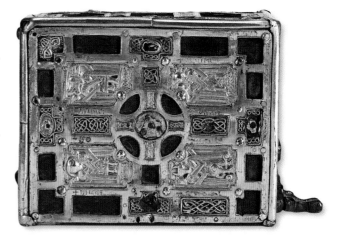

metal or die-cast and there was a concentration of such activity in the Christchurch Place area. Evidence of fine metalworking in Dublin has led to the suggestion by a number of scholars that some of Ireland's most important ecclesiastical treasures were made there in the early eleventh century. One example is the book-shrine known as the Soiscéal Molaise, a relic associated with St Molaise, a sixth-century saint from the island monastery of Devenish, Co. Fermanagh. This artefact demonstrates an impressive range of metalworking techniques and exquisite ornamentation.

Lead casting appears to have been common in Dublin workshops. Partly because of its low melting point, lead was easy to work and many of the inhabitants of Dublin seem to have tried their hand with it. The range of lead artefacts is extremely diverse and includes cross-shaped pendants, miniature anchors (serving as ornaments), plumb bobs and spindle whorls. Most significant from an archaeological perspective are the lead weights. It is possible that some of these were multiples of a standard Dublin weight unit, implying a regulated trading function. Other weights were line and net sinkers used by fishermen.

Most precious of all, of course, were gold and silver. The availability of gold in late tenth-century Dublin is hinted at in the annals for 989 when the high king, Máel Sechnaill II, allegedly imposed a tax of an ounce of gold per household, to be paid annually 'for ever'. It is possible that, sixteen years later, at least some of the twenty ounces of gold deposited by Brian Bórama on the altar of the main church at Armagh could have been derived from tributary payments by Dubliners to their newly acquired overlord. A quarter of a century further on, a ransom demanded by the men of Brega included sixty ounces each of gold and silver.

One other hard material, stone, appears to have had only a limited range of uses in Viking Dublin: for example, as conical gaming pieces, linen smoothers and whetstones for sharpening tools. The hearths of main dwelling houses were commonly defined by kerbstones, and paving stones or pebbles were sometimes used to floor corner compartments. The most spectacular use of stone came right at the end of our period – a town wall built from local, mottled-grey, calp

Above: Bronze key from Ellesø Skovsø, Copenhagen, Denmark. Keys are sometimes found in the furnished graves of women, reflecting their social standing as guardians in the household. Some keys would not have been useable and may have represented a symbolic statement.

Right: Front of the Soiscéal Molaise book-shrine. In the centre is a ringed cross with expanded terminals, the inset gold filigree providing settings for semi-precious stones. Four large panels contain symbols of the Evangelists, their Latin names engraved in the silver framework.

Dublin and the Viking World

limestone the construction of which has been dated archaeologically to *c.* 1100. Also belonging to later phases of the Viking Age are graveslabs found mainly in the Rathdown district, representing a distinctly Hiberno-Norse expression of Christian remembrance.

Animal Resources

Medieval craftsmen derived an enormous range of materials from slaughtered animals and very little was disposed of as waste. Only some animals were a source of food and many others were exploited for making useful things. Mammals' bones range widely in size and utility. At the larger end, the shin-bones of horses were converted into skates, perhaps as a cultural import from the Scandinavian homelands. At the smaller end, fine bones were commonly crafted into pins and needles, as an alternative to metal, as well as bone whistles whose musical capacity is uncertain.

Bones were also selected to try out decorative patterns for artwork, in the form of motif-pieces or trial-pieces. The Dublin excavations have yielded around 250 of these, representing by far the largest collection from a single location in Ireland. They exhibit stylistic traits of both Insular and Norse traditions, once again as expressions of an essentially mixed culture.

With regard to domestic animals, the cultural dominance of cattle as currency for socio-economic exchanges and as the preferred meat for human consumption was paralleled by the general availability of cow hides for leatherworking. The range of leather artefacts identified by archaeologists includes bags, belts, pouches or purses, satchels, shoes and straps, scabbards and sheaths. Technically a scabbard is a rigid holder for a weapon and could also be

Left: Gold armlets from High Street, Dublin, *c.* 1000. The Thór's ring confiscated from the Dubliners by King Máel Sechnaill II in 995 could have been an oath-swearing armband of some kind like these armlets. This high-class pair of personal adornments was found together.

Right: Three Rathdown graveslabs displayed on the church wall at Rathmichael, Co. Dublin. All grave markers of this type found so far come from south of the River Liffey, arguably the original heartland of the Scandinavian kingdom of Dublin.

Bone motif-piece from Dublin. Motif-pieces are an Insular and mainly Irish find type, perhaps representing apprentices' learning attempts. Their occurrence in Scandinavia after *c.* 1000 suggests that they arrived there from the west via Dublin or London.

A pair of woollen mittens discovered in 1960 by a farmer in Heynes, western Iceland. The mittens are made of composite woven wool and a strap. Norsemen settled in Iceland, where freezing temperatures encouraged the development of high-quality textiles.

made from wood, whereas a sheath is semi-flexible and could be used for tools as well as for weapons. Research has shown that until *c.* 980 the characteristics of both scabbards and sheaths are wholly Viking; thereafter northern European types are accompanied by local imitations of them in what can reasonably be regarded as the Hiberno-Norse period.

Most of Ireland's early Vikings originated in Norway, where the long winter months are cold. In such conditions, clothing made from fur-bearing animals was a necessity rather than a luxury. It is highly probable that there was an active fur trade, though the archaeological evidence for it is slight. Wild badgers, foxes and even the occasional wolf offered possibilities for pelts, and the skins of domestic and feral cats may have been used to line the inside of gloves. Seal skin, a much tougher type of skin, was cut into narrow strips and probably used for ships' rigging and ropes.

The Dublin excavations have produced over two thousand combs or comb parts. Combs were valued personal items, their teeth often protected by cases, and they were used not only for hair but also for beards. They were normally made from the antler of the red deer, an animal that must have abounded in the Wicklow mountains to the south. Every spring, antlers were shed naturally, providing a regular and easily accessible supply. Most of the Dublin combs are composite, constructed from thin plates of antler from which the teeth were cut before being clamped between two side plates which were then riveted together. These side plates were commonly decorated with simple, abstract, geometrical designs.

One of the great creatures of the northern seas was the walrus, whose tusks provided another raw material for expert craft-working. Around forty pieces of walrus 'ivory' have turned up in Dublin excavations, mainly in the Christchurch

FINDS BOX

Leatherworking

Animal skins were traditionally converted to leather by the removal of non-fibrous proteins and the addition of vegetable tannins. Tanning leather needed a regular supply of fresh water, which in turn dictated the location of such workshops. Obnoxious smells were associated with the process and later medieval records suggest that tanneries were kept at a distance from residential areas.

Altogether more than 5500 leather finds have been recorded from the National Museum of Ireland's excavation campaign, many of them dating from Viking Age levels. The anaerobic (that is, airless) burial environment around Wood Quay was particularly favourable to their preservation. While the full assemblage of leather artefacts and workshop debris from Dublin has not yet been published in detail, a lot of research has been conducted on scabbards and sheaths.

Scabbards for larger blades such as swords and daggers contained only the blade, leaving the hilt exposed. Sword scabbards were stiffened inside with wood to protect the weapon from damage and the wearer from injury, and lined with skin or textile. Four of the Dublin scabbards carry incised designs considered to be graffiti.

Sheaths enclosed both the blade and the handle of small knives that were carried for personal use, suspended from a belt by a carrying strap. They were made from a single piece of leather, seamed either along the edge corresponding to the knife blade, in the Anglo-Saxon tradition, or up the back face. Moulding (that is, the shaping of wet leather and then clamping it until dry) is commonly found on decorated sheaths of the tenth and eleventh centuries, adding strength and stiffness to the sheath.

Knife sheath from Christchurch Place, Dublin, third quarter of the eleventh century. This example bears the intriguing Latin inscription +EDRIC ME FECI[T], 'Eadric made me', the English name being indicative of a late Anglo-Saxon connection.

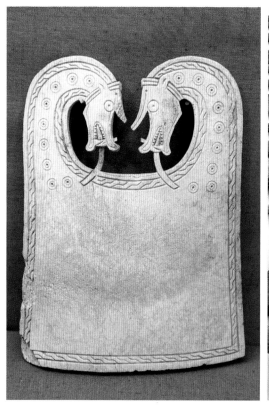

Left: Whalebone plaque found in the small boat burial on Sanday Island, Orkney, Scotland. Comparable to a modern ironing board, these plaques were used to straighten clothing using a round glass stone. Others have been discovered in the Viking world, including Dublin.

Right: Selection of deer antler off-cuts from York. In Dublin, antler was utilised with considerable effect during the Viking Age. Soaking antler softens the bone temporarily, allowing craftspeople to shape the material and create robust and functional everyday items.

Place area – the richest so far identified. One eleventh-century workshop there was using both antler and walrus ivory for making gaming pieces. Nothing as exquisite as the chessmen found on the island of Lewis in the Outer Hebrides has yet been discovered in Dublin, though chess, a game of Indian origin transmitted to western Europe via Russia and Scandinavia, was certainly being played there.

Cloth Production

According to the *Oxford English Dictionary*, the word 'craftswoman' is rare, yet in the Viking Age women made things just as men did. Girls inherited from their mother and other adult females a number of practicalities and were usually set to work around the farm or town house at an early age. It was essential for women to be able to make clothes, which required a wide range of skills.

Processes connected with the production of cloth can leave archaeological traces. A line of loom weights a short distance from the inner wall of a building

may indicate the presence of a loom for weaving. Early medieval looms consisted of a wooden frame leaning at a slight angle against a wall. The weaver worked in a standing position, having suspended the vertical threads forming the warp from a bar at the top before inserting the weft or woof at right-angles with the aid of a boat-shaped shuttle which held a further supply of woollen thread. Weaving cloth in this way required concentration, skill and stamina.

Prior to weaving, wool needed to be processed by carding and spinning. Wooden carding implements have been found, as have copper-alloy and wooden spindles. Spindle whorls come in a variety of materials, including bone, chalk, clay, jet and stone, as well as in different shapes and weights. After weaving, the finishing processes, such as fulling (cleaning and thickening cloth by treading it in a vat of liquid) and dyeing in vats and drying on tenterhooks, leave fewer archaeological traces. A more refined, small-scale type of work is known as tablet weaving, carried out on a board 30–40 mm square. Silk braids woven in this way are likely to have been imported as exotic and highly desirable items.

Above: Female clothing reconstructed on the basis of a grave in Finland and representing early eleventh-century fashion. All of the articles of clothing are of wool, dyed naturally, while the chain decorations, round brooches and spiral-ornamented apron are distinctly Finnish.

Above left: Reconstruction of a woman weaving at a vertical loom. An important hand-held tool was the weaver's sword, a blade-like wooden implement wielded by the woman in order to guide and compress the horizontal weft into position.

Left: Bone, horn and wooden weaver's tablets from Christchurch Place and Fishamble Street, Dublin. Narrow bands of cloth or braids would have had a wide range of uses, such as for trimming the edges of garments and wearing as hair ribbons.

For cloth production an alternative to wool was linen made from flax stalks. Flax was grown near or even in Dublin and was certainly being processed there prior to its use in weaving. The stalks needed to be retted (softened by soaking) before being dried, broken with wooden mallets, scutched with wooden blades and then drawn through combs with iron teeth known as hackles. All of this would have been typically the work of women, as is indicated by an early Irish text that accords to a divorcee a whole series of flax-related entitlements.

As in other cultures, women and children in the Viking Age undertook a wide range of other domestic duties around both rural farm and urban household. Cows, sheep and goats were milked, and curds and whey turned into cheese and butter respectively, as well as into what was regarded as a nourishing drink called buttermilk. Fowl were fed and managed, their eggs being a regular source of food. It goes without saying that most meals were prepared and cooked on fires that had to be kept alight. Judging by later medieval custom, the making of ale was a cottage industry pursued for the most part by women, hence the Middle English term 'alewife'. Indeed, the essentials of life in northern latitudes – food and drink, clothing and shelter – owed a great deal to the care and fortitude of women.

Dublin and the Viking World

FINDS BOX

Viking Art

The origins of Viking art lie in prehistoric Germanic art, and animal ornamentation was a key element immediately before and throughout the Viking period, with figural and narrative art featuring to a lesser extent.

The earliest of the six main Viking styles is the Oseberg, prevalent in the first three-quarters of the ninth century. The Oseberg style is typified by textured carpet patterns made up of squat animals rendered in relief, often gripping the frames with their paws. It is found carved on wooden items in the remarkable Oseberg ship burial, excavated in south-eastern Norway in 1904. Its successor was the Borre style, named for the decoration on a set of mounts from a ship burial in Vestfold, Norway, the principal element of which was a novel and lively gripping beast. Borre style was popular throughout Scandinavia during the tenth century and was the first to make an impact in areas of Viking influence outside the homelands.

Overlapping with the Borre style was the Jellinge style, deeply rooted in the Germanic tradition classified by George Salin. This style is named after a gilt and nielloed silver cup found in a mid-tenth-century royal burial mound at Jelling in Denmark. The decoration on the cup features a pair of intertwined S-shaped animals, shown in profile with evenly shaped ribbon bodies, spiral hip joints, circular eyes, open jaws and a distinctive long mane.

The ensuing, more innovative Mammen style takes its name from the designs inlaid on an iron axe from a late tenth-century grave in Denmark, one side of which bears a new foliate design of fleshy tendrils with hooked ends and the other face occupied by a muscular contorted bird with a robust shell spiral hip, both treated with surface pelleting.

Above: One of five animal-head posts of unknown function from the Oseberg ship burial, Norway. They are considered to be the work of different hands from a single workshop. This post was made by a technical and precise sculptor working in low relief.

Left: Cast silver open-work pendant with a Borre-style design of a gripping beast, four protruding animal heads, surface gilding and niello. Found in Little Snoring, Norfolk, the pendant is very similar to six found in the Vårby hoard of central Sweden.

Above: Small silver cup with gilded interior from the chamber grave in the north mound at Jelling, Denmark. The chamber was probably constructed for King Gorm c. 958/9. The ornamentation comprises a pair of intertwined animals with ribbon bodies, inlaid with black niello for contrast.

Above: Iron parade axe with silver inlay excavated from a richly furnished grave at Mammen, Denmark. On one side is a foliate pattern, on the other a bird with a round eye, a head crest and a shell-spiral hip. Both designs are filled with distinctive pellets.

Above: Detail of the weather-vane from Heggen church in Norway, decorated in fine Ringerike style. On one side, the design has a bird in combat with a snake. The other side shows a quadruped fighting with a sinuous creature.

Other favourite Mammen motifs include a human mask with interlaced beard and a great beast, a muscular quadruped with a backward-looking head, as found on the casket of walrus ivory from Bamberg Cathedral.

Two art styles, Ringerike and Urnes, originated in the 'runestone style' of southern Sweden and flourished consecutively during the eleventh century in Scandinavia, towards the end of the Viking Age. The earlier to emerge was the Ringerike style, which takes its name from a group of memorial stones from the Oslo region and which drew extensively on western European art, making use of vegetal ornament, the great beast and bird motifs. The Urnes style, which takes its name from carvings on a stave church in western Norway, was by contrast purely zoomorphic, drawing on the long tradition of animal forms in Germanic art, creating elegant compositions from the looping bodies of extremely stylised beasts and snakes. The Urnes style influenced Romanesque art and architecture in Scandinavia and in Ireland.

A unique phenomenon in the tenth century was the Gotlandic picture stones, which feature figural scenes, the meanings of which are mostly inscrutable. Some have been interpreted as narratives from legends, such as Völund the smith, or depicting Scandinavian cult practices. The Gotlandic stones and other items of figural ornamentation such as the Oseberg tapestry also hint at the potential for the lost art of the period. Christianity features in later Viking art, for example on the silver filigree-decorated crucifix pendant from Trondheim, Norway. There is also evidence for syncretism – the combining of seemingly contradictory beliefs – in the conversion period, as on the Gosforth and the Middleton crosses in northern England.

Right: Detail of the decoration on a small stave-built wooden church at Urnes, Norway. These remarkably preserved panels date to the second half of the eleventh century. A scene showing an elegant beast in combat with snakes and other creatures is superbly carved in high relief.

6

At Home with the Vikings

Even true Vikings did not spend most of their time as sea-pirates; instead, their everyday life revolved around settlements and homesteads in a mostly rural environment

Vikings were homebirds at heart. In Old Norse, the word *heim* meant 'home' or 'homewards' and *heiman* 'from home'. These words are found frequently in the later saga literature, where the noun *heimr*, 'abode' is used in both earthly and mythological contexts. Harsh, long winters, especially in Norway and Sweden, called for careful preparation and skilled house-building for survival. House types were determined by the availability of raw materials and modified by climatic factors and by cultural traditions. In most parts of Scandinavia, timber was plentiful and widely used for houses and ancillary buildings. Settlement abroad brought other factors into play, including the native building traditions in Ireland, Britain and northern France, and challenging environmental conditions in the North Atlantic colonies.

According to later literature a distinctive Nordic way of dealing with an enemy was to burn him and his household alive in their house. This custom was called *brenna inni*, 'to burn in', most famously in the story of Burnt Njál.

The Viking House

An early type of Scandinavian house, known as the longhouse, was bow-sided. This is represented archaeologically by post-holes for both the main sidewalls and their external supports. Evidence for curved walls and shingled roofs comes from shaped gravestones (hogbacks) found mostly in England and Scotland, and from relic shrines like the Cammin casket – a curved wooden box covered in elk horn plaques dating to *c.* 1000 – and from houses pictured on tapestry. A longhouse of this form measuring 24 m was discovered during excavations at Oma in Rogaland, Norway, dating to *c.* 950 and reconstructed at the museum at Avaldsnes Nordvegen Historiesenter.

In all cases the main room had a central hearth. This was the heart of a typical home, for cooking, heating and limited lighting in usually windowless rooms. On each long side of the hearth there would normally be low 'benches' for sitting, reclining and sleeping. Furs and tapestries would have covered the walls and helped to insulate the house and keep it warm. Smoke from the central fireplace escaped through a small covered hole in the roof above. Gradually bow-sided houses gave way to rectangular ones and there is evidence of a process of evolution from one multipurpose room to two or more rooms in line.

According to the sagas, an important man's seat in his house was flanked by poles endowed with symbolic significance. In *Landnámabók*, an Icelandic work describing the

Reconstruction of a house with wattle walls at Hedeby (Haithabu) in northern Germany. Built of timber felled in 870, this dwelling house had a main room flanked by a side room with a dome-shaped bread-oven and another devoted to craft-working.

settlement (*landnám*, 'land taking') of Iceland by Norsemen in the ninth and tenth centuries, some characters deliberately cast these poles overboard from their ship when seeking a landing place on which to set up a new home. Ancillary structures include the boathouse (Old Norse *naust*) with curved long walls and an open end towards the water for winter boat storage. A boathouse of this type was found at Leidang in Rogaland and reconstructed at Avaldsnes.

The most sophisticated dwelling houses that have been excavated so far had three principal components: a central hall with a workshop on one side and a byre for domestic animals on the other. The exceptionally well-preserved Viking chieftain's farmstead at Hrísbrú in Mosfell, east of Reykjavík in Iceland, had bow-sided long walls extending in length over 28 m, a central hall (probably wood-

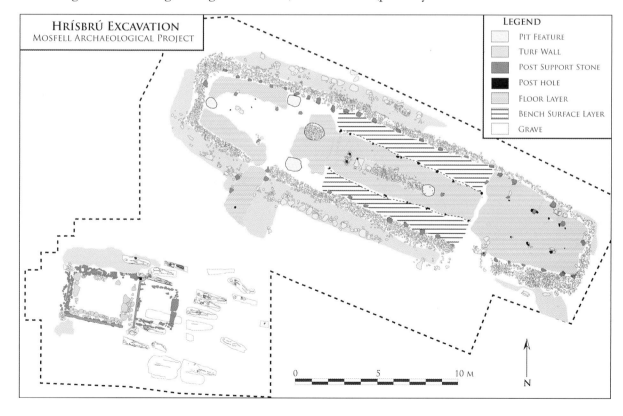

Left: Artist's reconstruction of the interior of a typical Dublin (Type 1) dwelling house of the Viking Age. Much can be learnt about diet and general living conditions from environmental archaeology. Floor surfaces seem to have been kept relatively clean.

Below: Plan of the farmstead at Hrísbrú, Iceland, in its later stage *c.* 1000. By then the small private church had been built nearby, around the time of general acceptance of Christianity in Iceland. Bow-sided house-building continued alongside rectangular structures.

HRÍSBRÚ EXCAVATION
MOSFELL ARCHAEOLOGICAL PROJECT

LEGEND

	PIT FEATURE
	TURF WALL
	POST SUPPORT STONE
	POST HOLE
	FLOOR LAYER
	BENCH SURFACE LAYER
	GRAVE

0   5   10 M

N

panelled), a room at the western end used mainly for the production of textiles, an antechamber to the hall itself, and a basic eastern gable room suitable for animals, storage and a workshop.

In the emerging urban environment of Viking Dublin, a quite different type of dwelling house was established from the beginning of the settlement in the second half of the ninth century. A typical Dublin house (known by archaeologists as Type 1) measured about 8.5 m long by 4.75 m wide. The low walls were made from post-and-wattle with rounded corners and did not bear the roof weight. The roof structure rested on four vertical posts. The normal roofing materials were probably straw thatch on top of sod under-layering. Over two hundred Viking Age houses of this and related forms have been discovered in Dublin. So uniform are these houses that it would seem that 'professional' house-builders were being employed.

There were numerous smaller buildings such as the Type 2 house. Other structures probably functioned as outhouses, workshops, sheds for animals, and latrines. One of the most striking features of all these buildings is that they are entirely organic in terms of the materials used. Dublin's biggest secular building was presumably the royal hall, whose location and nature are unknown. A likely site is that of the later castle, overlooking the 'black pool' in the River Poddle that would have provided a secure haven for the all-important fleet of warships. This may be inferred from the Norsemen's decision to name the place Dyflinn (Irish Duiblinn, 'black pool') and the territorial district Dyflinnarskíri (Dublinshire).

Food and Drink

Before the age of containerised traffic and supermarkets, human diet tended to reflect the rural economy of each locality. In the Scandinavian homelands, domestic animals were usually the main farming resource. Thus cattle byres, sheep sheds, goat sheds and pigsties feature frequently as outbuildings on excavated sites. Summer pasturage on high ground (transhumance) was practised in some

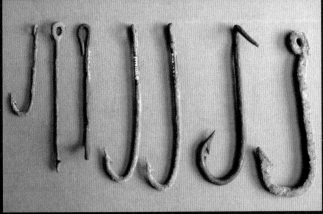

districts, such as Trøndelag in Norway and parts of Iceland. Hunting, trapping and netting wild animals and birds were normal activities and were conducted for food, raw materials and exports.

The homelands also abounded in seafood and river fish, with the result that fishing constituted a vital part of the rural economy. Though they leave little archaeological trace, fish-drying sheds with open slatted sides were probably common. In the far north, whales, walruses and seals were caught for their oil for lighting houses, for their hides and ivory, and for their skins. The *Annals of Ulster* for 828 record 'a great slaughter of porpoises on the coast of Ard Ciannachta [possibly Clogher Head, Co. Louth] by the foreigners'. One of the few completely Norse names in the Dublin area is Leixlip, from Old Norse *lax-hleypa*, 'salmon's leap'. By contrast, fishing was a minor part of the Irish economy and diet.

In more southerly areas inhabited or colonised by Scandinavians, including Ireland, a better-balanced diet could be based partly on vegetables such as beans and cabbage. Wild garlic and leeks were available seasonally, as well as a variety of herbs for both food and medicine. Most fruit consumed, whether in the countryside or in a town, was collected from the wild, as were nuts. The archaeology of Viking

Age Dublin has produced evidence for the consumption of apples, bilberries, blackberries and sloes. Analysis of the faunal remains indicates that about ninety percent of the meat was derived from cattle, brought in from farms in the surrounding countryside.

The commonest alcoholic drink in the Viking world was ale (Old Norse *öl*) made from barley. The barley grain is hardier than wheat and was grown together with oats, the latter for porridge for humans and fodder for horses. Lacking the hops that flavour beer, medieval ale was probably not to modern taste, but the saga literature implies that it was standard fare. Where conditions were favourable, mead made from fermenting a mixture of honey and water would have been an alternative. There are stories of heavy drinking sessions: in an incident in *Egil's Saga* a henchman sent forward to spy out the land reports back that he came across a servant who was blind drunk (*ölóðr*).

Weddings in particular were an occasion for a big feast or *veizla* in Old Norse. The plural of this word, *veizlur*, meant a nobleman's entitlement to receive hospitality from lesser landowners. We are rarely told by later written sources what foodstuffs and drinks constituted a feast, but the harvest would have been an obvious time of year to hold a celebration. The antechamber of the central hall at Hrísbrú was apparently used to display the household's store of food; invited guests would have assumed that they were in for a good feed.

Health and Hygiene

When we start to get reasonably reliable indications of human life expectancy in Europe, in thirteenth-century England, the stark reality is that the *average* male could expect to live into his early thirties. The archaeological and literary evidence suggests that Viking warriors were young men who were likely to die in battle, and skeletons excavated near the pool of Dublin show as much. On the other hand, the violent saga character Egill Skallagrímsson lived into his eighties. The high-status female buried at Finglas was of childbearing age. The greatest risk to women's health was childbirth.

One of the abiding impressions to be derived from Old Icelandic literature of a later age is how physically fit and vigorous Vikings are portrayed. Fighting

Location maps of the Finglas burial. As elsewhere, this grave was positioned outside the core of the ecclesiastical settlement dedicated to St Canice, representing some kind of social or religious accommodation between Christianity and paganism in the Viking Age.

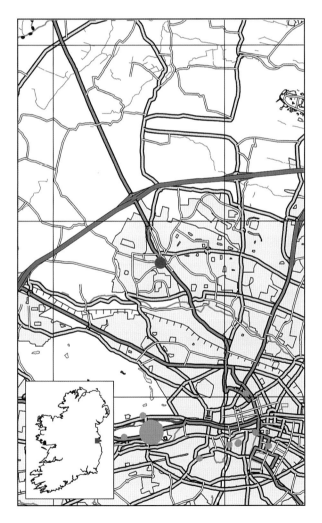

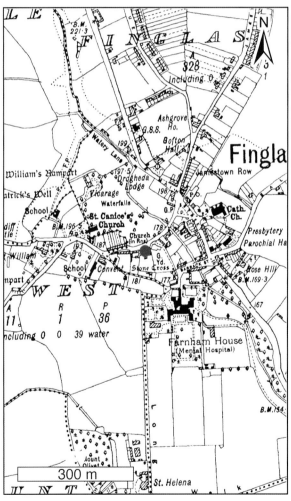

on foot, sometimes on board a moving vessel at sea, required agility, comparable perhaps with that of a modern lightweight boxer. The sword, the principal weapon for high-status warriors, had a blade about 80 cm long, the tang (the piece which supports the hilt) adding a further 10 cm. It was designed as a slashing instrument for use in one hand.

A feature of all early medieval cultures was that there was little or no obesity, partly because of regular physical activity. One exception was the earl of Orkney killed at Clontarf in 1014, known as Sigur∂r the Stout. The absence of refined sugar in people's diet meant that dental caries were comparatively rare. On the other hand the low status female skeleton exhibited in Dublinia had poor oral health, including tooth loss and chronic abscesses, during her lifetime in the twelfth century. The much earlier (*c.* 800) best-preserved warrior found at South Great George's Street, still in the prime of life when he died, suffered from serious back problems caused possibly by heavy labour in childhood.

The legendary Sigur∂r slaying the dragon, depicted on a portal of the stave church at Hylestad, Norway. In the Viking world view, Sigur∂r was a heroic figure whose bravery and invincibility made his name popular and commonly found in saga literature.

Waste disposal was a constant problem, as it remains to this day. Animals and humans were sources of waste material that had to be managed carefully so as to avoid disease. In the countryside farmers could use some of this waste as fertiliser, but townspeople living in crowded conditions had to find other disposal solutions. A common feature found on excavations is the cesspit, dug usually in the back garden of the property plot. The corner units of Dublin Type 1 houses may have contained some sort of commode that could be emptied into the cesspit after use. Moss and other soft vegetable matter were used in the same way as toilet paper.

Medieval people of all classes were prone to fleas and lice because of living conditions and the comb was an important item for grooming hair and beards. It was impossible to heat large quantities of water in order to wash bedding, clothing and the human body. Plant matter, spread deliberately on the floor of a Dublin house, would have provided a measure of insulation and a barrier from the damp. Scavengers, including vermin, were commonplace and spread disease. The cleanest Vikings were probably those who happened to live near one of Iceland's natural geysers, where regular bathing was possible even in midwinter. The best alternative was the steam bathhouse with a flagged floor where hot stones would be drenched in cold water, like a sauna.

Dress and Lifestyle

Archaeological excavation has produced evidence for dress, including fragments of cloth of different kinds as well as dress fittings and personal ornaments. Costume would have varied with social status and cultural background. Standard male attire was a shirt and trousers worn under a tunic and cloak. Viking women typically wore a long woollen overdress with a woollen or linen shift or smock underneath. Cotton was unknown in northern Europe in the Viking Age, ruling out comfortable underwear. Roughest of all were the garments worn by male and female slaves.

Some of the most unusual items of dress from the Dublin excavations are the head coverings worn by women and possibly men. Some of these were fitted caps with ties for fastening under the chin or behind the head; others were headbands and scarves. Veils of light woollen or fine silk fabric belonged to women of the uppermost social levels, the silks being imported ready-woven from or via Byzantium (modern Istanbul) and often dyed in bright reds, blues or purple with natural pigments. The woollen examples were generally undyed but still of high quality and perhaps produced in local workshops.

Dresses and cloaks were fastened at the shoulders by brooches or pins. The

Different ways of wearing head scarves in the Viking Age. Ten wool and six silk pieces of cloth of the scarf type have been found in the Dublin excavations. Fashion determined methods of wearing such garments to the best effect.

Two ringed pins, a copper-alloy belt buckle and a possible weaving implement from Dublin. Before buttons were adopted, brooches and pins were normally used to fasten clothing. Belts were for small personal items such as combs, keys, knives and purses.

pagan burial grounds have yielded a number of pairs of brooches. The simplest dress fastener was the ringed-pin, adopted by Vikings from the Irish in the ninth century. Nearly three hundred of these pins, mostly of copper alloy, have been discovered in Dublin. For fastening purposes the pin of the ringed-pin was bent slightly in the middle and fixed diagonally upwards in the fabric, and in some cases tied off with thread. Polished bone stick-pins, some carved with animal or bird heads, may have been hair ornaments.

Gold foil or simulated gold foil beads and one ring bead from Dunmore Cave. In 930 Dublin Vikings massacred a large number of people at Dunmore, perhaps to undermine an alliance between Osraige (Ossory) and the Vikings of Limerick.

Ornamental brooches are found in a variety of types – including Anglo-Saxon-style disc brooches, Celtic-style penannular brooches, and thistle- and kite-shaped brooches which are Insular-Viking hybrids. Each of these types has a unique geographical and chronological range. Another common statement of identity was beads made from precious and semi-precious materials. Nine glass beads were found in the limestone caves at Dunmore in Co. Kilkenny. Six of seven found together featured gold foil (made of true and simulated gold) and all nine are thought to represent a single personal ornament. Beads of this type would have been imported from elsewhere in the Viking world and those at Dunmore, a place known to Vikings, are thought to have been deposited there in the late tenth century.

Gaming board found at Ballinderry *crannóg*, Co. Westmeath. The ring-chain pattern is a West Viking variant of the tenth-century Borre art style. The board was perhaps made in Dublin or Limerick. A popular game of attack and defence was called *hnefatafl*.

Work probably took up most of the time of all able-bodied men, women and older children during the spring, summer and autumn: survival depended on preparation for the next winter, especially in the Scandinavian homelands and in the North Atlantic colonies. During the long, severe winters there, people were mainly confined to windowless houses lit by the hearth fire and by oil-lamps. A common archaeological find is the gaming piece, including chessmen. Story-telling and saga recitation ranked highly as winter pastimes; many sagas are ancestral tales set in a known and familiar physical environment. We can imagine them being composed, told and retold by people sitting on those benches either side of a central hearth.

At Home with the Vikings

FINDS BOX

Castle Street, Dublin

Excavations in the 1990s at 26–29 Castle Street and 20 Lord Edward Street revealed the foundations of a number of houses concentrated in the southern half of the site. The house sequence dates from the late tenth century (the time of King Sigtryggr Silkenbeard) to the second half of the twelfth century (the time of the Anglo-Norman conquest).

This area was first occupied when the town was being consolidated by Sigtryggr, following on from his father Óláfr Kvaran, and the population was expanding. The plots and houses were generally wider than those at Fishamble Street, suggesting the possibility of higher social status, which makes sense if the royal compound was on the site of the later castle.

All of the buildings were rectangular in plan, measuring approximately 8.2 m by 5.5 m. Standard features were large posts to support the roof, a central hearth, side aisles, and doorways 1 m wide at the narrow northern and southern ends. These houses all had post-and-wattle side and end walls, except for one that incorporated stave-built side walls. Many had sharp bones deliberately woven into the lowest strand of wattle, which may have been placed there to prevent rodents from gnawing at the walls.

The foundation remains of the largest (9 m by 6 m) building at Castle Street date from the mid-eleventh century, around the time when the town started to come under Irish control. It had a plank-furnished floor inside the south doorway, incorporating reused ships' timbers. The large amount of waste material indicated that this was an amber workshop. Altogether around three thousand pieces of amber were discovered during the Wood Quay excavations, the second highest concentration of any Viking settlement excavated in Europe.

Archaeologists excavating a wattle structure found at Castle Street, Dublin. Most of the pits from this site were unlined, but some were lined with pre-prepared wattle and others with horizontal timber planks. Note the protective helmets worn by the workers.

The Castle Street excavation site in 1993 with a Viking house and wooden pathway in the centre and towards the right. Many wattle houses had sharp bones woven into the lowest sections, possibly to deter rodents from gnawing the walls.

Dublin and the Viking World

7

Viking Towns

Vikings as raiders were not necessarily town dwellers, but their trading activities led to the development of some of Ireland's most important medieval towns

Vikings operating and settling in Ireland are normally credited with five town foundations – Cork, Dublin, Limerick, Waterford and Wexford – each of which had a different origin and evolved in a different way. Of these, Dublin, though not an original Viking town, was undoubtedly the most important and remained so for the rest of the Middle Ages and beyond. In early ninth-century Scandinavia there were three trading settlements with town-like characteristics under Danish control: Hedeby (now Haithabu) in northern Germany, Kaupang in southern

Norway and Ribe in western Denmark. By the end of the Viking Age, *c.* 1100, the first two of these had been abandoned and replaced on alternative sites. Town foundation in Scandinavia during the Viking Age was a hesitant and uncertain process, lacking the charter-based models of later times. The same was true of Ireland, where the bigger ecclesiastical centres (monasteries) came to have some typical urban features associated with craft-working and trading, yet they were orientated primarily towards religious devotion and observance.

Life before Towns

Across northern Europe in the early Viking Age, most people lived in a do-it-yourself world of self-sufficiency in which towns were a rarity. Town life has become so dominant in our own times that it is difficult now to imagine a world without towns. Even in southern England and northern France, where there were some towns, most of the inhabitants of what came to be 'the Viking world' lived a life of rustic frugality on a farm or in a hamlet or village. They engaged in field cultivation, managed domestic animals, hunted for wild ones, fished in rivers and the sea, cut timber for construction, hearths and furnaces, and quarried for metal ores and stone.

Reconstruction of a *ráth* or farmstead in the Irish National Heritage Park. Thousands of such sites survive even now as circular earthworks whose wooden palisades and interior farm buildings have long since disappeared. 'Rath' is a common place-name element.

In the context of Britain and Ireland at the beginning of the Viking Age, the exception was England. Much earlier, Romans had created an extensive network of towns and trading settlements, many of them well fortified and interlinked by an infrastructure of roads and river crossings. By the end of the fifth century,

Map artwork by Anú Design (www.anu-design.ie)

THE TOWNS OF ROMAN BRITAIN

- ● Colonia
- ● Civitas capital
- ○ Failed civitas capital
- ● Other fortified vicus
- ○ Undefended vicus
- ∿ Margin of the highland zone

Map of the towns of Roman Britain, most of which were situated in the lowland zone. When town life revived in the seventh century, former Roman sites were reused together with new ones. The place-name elements 'cester' and 'chester' are clues.

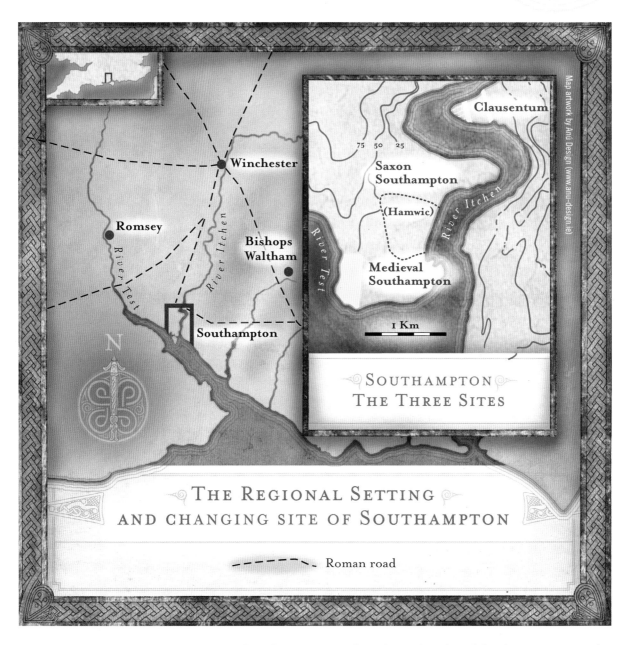

Map artwork by Anú Design (www.anu-design.ie)

Clausentum

75 50 25

Saxon Southampton

(Hamwic)

Medieval Southampton

River Test

River Itchen

1 Km

SOUTHAMPTON
THE THREE SITES

Winchester

Romsey

Bishops Waltham

River Test

River Itchen

Southampton

N

THE REGIONAL SETTING
AND CHANGING SITE OF SOUTHAMPTON

– – – – – Roman road

The regional setting and changing site of Southampton. Roman *Clausentum* was replaced by Hamwic, which in turn started to migrate to the site of the medieval walled town in the mid-ninth century. Hamwic served as the port of Winchester.

however, even London appears to have been abandoned for the most part and it was not until the seventh century that there was a significant revival of trading across the North Sea and along the English Channel. A number of trading settlements, called by modern scholars 'emporia', emerged with place-names ending in *–wic* (from Latin *vicus*, 'settlement'): for example, Eoforwic (York), Gipeswic (Ipswich), Hamwic (Southampton) and Lundenwic (London).

Dublin and the Viking World

Modern place-names in England which contain this element include Berwick and Warwick.

The development of these settlements in England would have become known in Scandinavia, particularly in Denmark. Accordingly, when Danish Vikings began their concerted campaigns in England in the 840s, an important aspect of their strategy was to attack towns and trading settlements, just as they did in northern France. The decade opened with an assault on Southampton, where its local governor (*ealdorman*) defeated the crews of more than thirty ships. Two years later it was the turn of London and Rochester. In 851 both Canterbury and London were stormed by a much larger force and a subsequent engagement took place at Sandwich in Kent. Yet another established town, Winchester, was targeted in 860.

Scale model of the main monastic site at Glendalough, Co. Wicklow as it may have looked in the eleventh century. Inside the double enclosure, monks devoted themselves to religious observances and tenant farmers to life support. Trading took place outside the extant gateway.

From a Viking perspective, Ireland was a radically different prospect. The biggest centres of population and concentrations of movable wealth were not towns but major ecclesiastical settlements. This has given rise to the concept of 'monastic towns', a subject much debated by archaeologists and historians, partly because of the difficulty of determining what constituted a 'town' in this early period. Examples include Armagh, Clonmacnoise, Downpatrick, Glendalough, Kildare, Trim and Tuam. Some of these places did indeed eventually become genuine towns, but only after Anglo-Norman intervention in the late twelfth century. Before then, their essentially religious life was sustained by a support system that shared to some extent that of both the village and the town.

Along with northern England and the whole of Scotland and Wales, Ireland in the early Middle Ages is best regarded as a land with a minimal trend towards urbanisation. At the great monastic centres in Ireland, craft-working and marketing were secondary activities conducted outside the sacred core of the settlement. One achievement of the Vikings in Ireland, with long-lasting consequences, was to further that trend towards urban growth. Scandinavian trading both preceded and coincided with Scandinavian raiding, lending to the Viking world one of its most enduring qualities – that the exchange of goods and ideas came to be as natural to Vikings as to their contemporaries.

Trading Settlements

Trading settlements first appear in Iron Age, non-Roman Europe as small, undefended concentrations of people who may have had a nearby hilltop fortification as a place of refuge. The Latin word *vicus* and its Germanic equivalent *wic(h)* are associated with some of these. Direct access by means of water transportation, by sea or by river, was a universal characteristic and long-distance trade an economic driving force behind the emergence of these settlements.

One outstanding example of the early Viking Age has already been mentioned – Hedeby, near the southern end of the Jutland peninsula – about which most of our knowledge is archaeological. Hedeby appears to have begun as at least three loosely associated nuclei, each with a cemetery, which were settled from the start by craftsmen and merchants. Its central nucleus originated *c.* 811 and the greater part of the excavated area was occupied by the 830s. Hedeby developed near the meeting-point of different ethnic groups – Germans, Scandinavians and Slavs – as well as at the crossing-place between the North Sea and the Baltic Sea. Already in the ninth century, it would have been well known to traders operating in the Viking world.

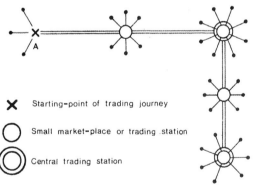

✕ Starting-point of trading journey

◯ Small market-place or trading station

◎ Central trading station

Above: Model of the relation between trade routes and market-places. Trading in early medieval Europe linked isolated beaches, small harbours with little infrastructure and internationally recognised centres. Viking Age Dublin became a major trading centre, initially on the basis of slave trading.

Right: Reconstruction of the tenth-century waterfront at Hedeby (Haithabu), northern Germany. Wooden houses of a Scandinavian type, distinctly different from the Dublin ones, front on to a series of jetties at which several single-masted merchant ships are moored for trading purposes.

Dublin and the Viking World

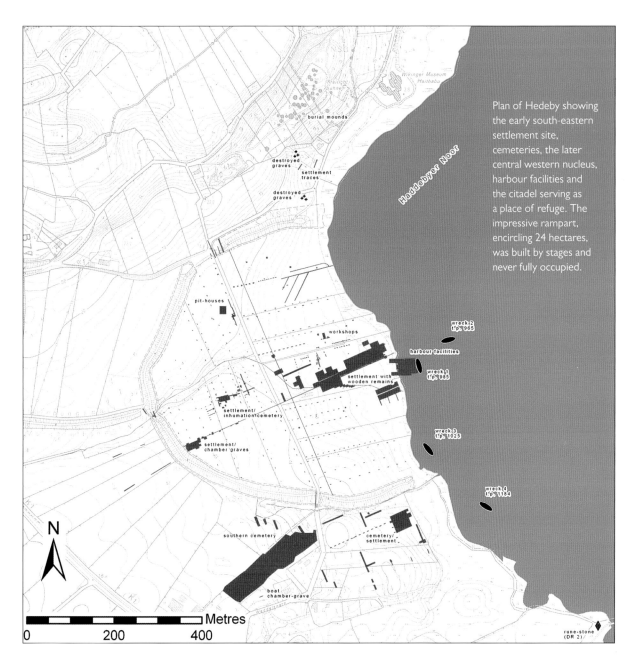

Plan of Hedeby showing the early south-eastern settlement site, cemeteries, the later central western nucleus, harbour facilities and the citadel serving as a place of refuge. The impressive rampart, encircling 24 hectares, was built by stages and never fully occupied.

Danes seem to have established a comparable trading settlement in what we call Norway, at Kaupang on the western shore of Oslofjord. During the first few years of its existence from *c.* 800, Kaupang was occupied only seasonally. Permanent habitation and plot division have been discovered only in parts of the excavated areas, while on the periphery craft-workers and merchants spent

Left: Plan of Kaupang
showing the distinction
between areas of
permanent and of
seasonal settlement. Only
a small proportion of this
mainly rural site has been
excavated to date, even
though archaeological
investigations began there in
the mid-nineteenth century.

Right: Summary
interpretation of features
at Annagassan, Co. Louth
revealed by geophysical
survey. Like Hedeby and
Kaupang, this is a classic site
that would repay research
excavation. Its brief period
of occupation in the ninth
century is comparable with
that at Woodstown, Co.
Waterford.

the summer months living in tents. Kaupang's population has been estimated variously at between 230 and 830 inhabitants, including children and slaves, all of which suggests that its urban status was always marginal at best.

Marginally urban though they may have been in the first decades of the ninth century, nothing like Hedeby or Kaupang existed in Ireland at that time. The contribution of the Vikings, therefore, was to make any trend towards urbanisation less minimal than it was before. A world of small, sometimes seasonal, trading settlements accessible by ocean-going ships would have been familiar to some Norwegians. Warrior merchants were necessarily mobile, as the archaeological discoveries of balance scales and ring money testify.

In the course of time, during the tenth and eleventh centuries, a small number of sites in Ireland acquired an urban identity, in which local and international trading were major components. Trading in itself, even in Ireland, was a long-standing occupation, but doing it in a real town was novel. The original model everywhere may have been the beach market, and this continued to be the case in Viking Iceland and elsewhere. The lack of high-cost infrastructural arrangements involved in holding a market on a beach could have been a financial advantage in an age of considerable insecurity and low economic productivity. Towns such as Dublin were different and came to make a difference.

Dublin Becomes a Town

Over the course of what is known as the *longphort* phase of Viking Dublin (841–902), this trading settlement became the Irish equivalent of Kaupang. Another trading settlement established at exactly the same time, Annagassan in Co. Louth, appears to have been abandoned by the Vikings in or soon after 852. One reason for this may have been that it could not compete successfully with Dublin, given the latter's command of four of the five main highways across the island. These highways gave overland access on horseback to wealth in various forms – gold, silver, horses, cows and especially human captives, male and female, for ransom or for sale.

The trading wealth of Dublin at the beginning of the tenth century is witnessed most clearly in the biggest Viking Age hoard ever found in western Europe, near Preston in Lancashire in north-western England. Known as the Cuerdale hoard, it is believed to have been deposited in its leaden chest *c.* 905, a few years after the enforced exile of the Dublin elite in 902. One theory is that it was intended to be used as a war chest to pay for mercenaries to assist

Below left: Part of the great Cuerdale silver hoard, weighing around 40 kg and found by chance discovery buried in the bank of the River Ribble. One positive aspect of Viking activity in Ireland was to increase the supply of silver.

Below right: Diagrammatic representation of the early tenth-century layout of buildings and access ways at Essex Street West, Dublin. The built environment was less regular than it later became, both here and along the western frontage of nearby Fishamble Street.

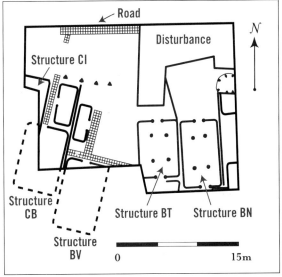

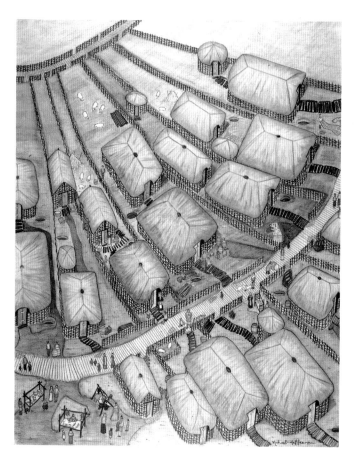

Artist's reconstruction of the plot division at Fishamble Street, Dublin, in the late tenth century. Over the course of time, a more regular, 'urban' plot pattern developed and was adhered to thereafter. A mixture of classified building types is shown here.

in the recapture of such a lucrative trading settlement. This spectacular combination of around 1300 individual pieces of silver and 7000 foreign coins, many of the latter freshly minted in York, had presumably been accumulated as a result of slave trading.

Dublin was reoccupied by Vikings in 917 under the leadership of a grandson of the ninth-century king Ívarr the Boneless (d. 873). Archaeological evidence suggests that a new waterside settlement was established downstream from the ancient ford across the River Liffey. Initially it seems to have had an air of impermanence, with a succession of kings abandoning Dublin and going to England, especially to York. In the mid-tenth century both documents and archaeology start to indicate a more stable environment, coinciding with the reign of Óláfr Kvaran (945–80). In 944 the descriptive term *dún*, 'fortress' or 'stronghold', is used of Dublin for the first time and became normal thereafter.

At Wood Quay the first defensive embankment has been dated archaeologically to *c.* 950, suggesting that a better-defended site existed by that time.

Slave trading was probably still a major occupation and the raid on Kildare in 929 was apparently timed for St Brigid's Day to take advantage of the influx of pilgrims. The last great raid out of Viking Dublin occurred in 951, when Kells (Co. Meath) was taken over as a base and from it were taken cows, horses, gold and silver, as well as a large number of men. In reverse mode, starting in 936, periodic attacks on Dublin were made by Irish high kings and would-be high kings. Just as Leinster and Meath had been sources of plunder for the Dublin Vikings, so now did Viking Dublin become a major source of plunder for the Irish.

The decline of plundering in the second half of the tenth century suggests that an alternative, 'urban' economy had been growing. We have no secure means of measuring this change, though the evolving plot pattern at Fishamble Street hints at an intensification of habitation from the third quarter of that century. Another feature of the tenth-century economy was very slow monetisation, represented by generally small numbers of mainly English coins. Only towards the end of the century have three significant hoards of coins been found, at Castle Street and Werburgh Street. Dublin had evolved by stages from a trading settlement into a town, with regular craft-working and the beginnings of a money economy.

Urban Maturity

The long reign of Sigtryggr Silkenbeard (989–1036), a son of Óláfr Kvaran, proved to be a turning point in the history of Viking Dublin in a number of ways. Half-Norse and half-Irish by birth, he probably spoke both languages and presided over an increasingly mixed culture that modern scholars refer to as Hiberno-Norse. Another part of that culture was purely English (Anglo-Saxon),

Conjectural map of Dublin c. 1000. King Sigtryggr's Dublin comprised a fortified town between the Rivers Liffey and Poddle, an assembly site (Thingmót) and royal burial mounds located towards the bay, and a scattering of Christian churches outside the *dún*.

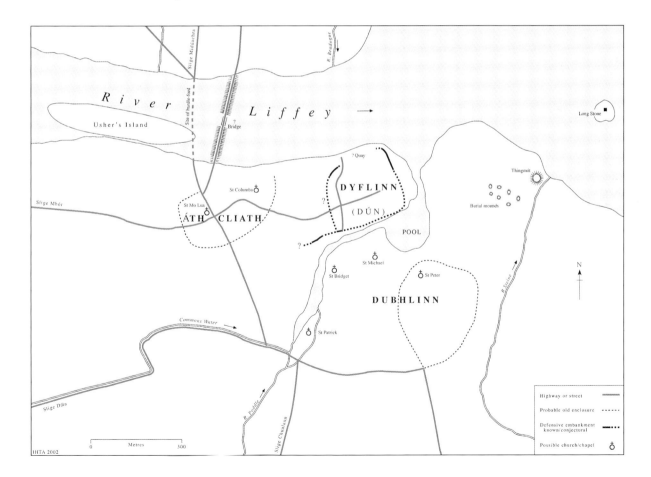

The eleventh-century Romanesque crypt of Christ Church Cathedral, Dublin, looking west. Built for both structural and ceremonial reasons, this is the oldest standing structure in central Dublin. Viking Age houses may have stood on the site beforehand, creating unstable ground conditions.

Opposite left: Dublin's Hiberno-Norse town wall, preserved inside the Wood Quay Venue. Dublin was one of the first towns north of the Alps to be surrounded by a defensive wall of stone since the Roman period. Quarrying, transportation and construction were expensive.

Opposite right: Successive building levels along the western side of Fishamble Street in the tenth and eleventh centuries. As might be expected in an unstable political environment, the density of building varied. The lifespan of such houses is estimated at twenty years.

hence his decision in the mid-990s to initiate a silver coinage modelled closely on that of contemporary England, which was already an important trading partner for Dublin's merchants. The first pennies, bearing Sigtryggr's portrait (without a beard), were probably made by professional moneyers brought over from England.

Another decision made late in the reign was to establish a Christian diocese based on the cathedral that we know as Christ Church, situated in what became the heart of the medieval city. This is believed to have happened soon after Sigtryggr's return from a pilgrimage to Rome in 1028. The early bishops of Hiberno-Norse Dublin were consecrated over in England by the archbishop of Canterbury and some of them had been trained as Benedictine monks in English monasteries. An unforeseen outcome of this was the interest shown in Dublin and in the Irish church in general by archbishops of Canterbury following the Norman conquest of England in and after 1066.

King Sigtryggr led a chequered political career in a highly unstable environment whose most dramatic turn of events was the great battle fought outside his town at Clontarf in 1014. Essentially the Dubliners had combined with the Leinstermen, supported by warriors from other parts of the Viking world, in rebellion against an assertive high king, Brian Bórama. Sigtryggr himself stayed inside the earth and timber defences as the commander of a protective garrison while most of the war leaders, including Brian, were killed in the bloodbath. But in the end, in 1036, Sigtryggr was deposed as king by a younger, Waterford-based rival and went into exile, probably to a small colonial outpost on Anglesey in north Wales.

The political scene changed again in 1052 when the king of Leinster, Diarmait mac Máel na mBó, took control of Dublin. He initiated a new policy whereby the most powerful provincial kings in Ireland, including recognised high kings, came to see control of Dublin as an essential component of their own political position. Having gained control, some of them installed their sons as governors, giving them practice in the art of ruling. Dubliners came to play an important part in eleventh-century political gamesmanship in Ireland.

Besides the cathedral, a number of other structures came to make Dublin more recognisably urban. It is possible, for example, that the ancient ford across the River Liffey was replaced by a wooden bridge right at the beginning of the century. The archaeology of Fishamble Street in particular has revealed a denser concentration of houses and workshops. Smaller churches were established, including St Olave's in the same street and, towards the end of the century, St Michan's in a northside suburb. Most impressive of all would have been the stone defensive wall encircling the town, built from local calp limestone blocks and dated archaeologically to *c.* 1100.

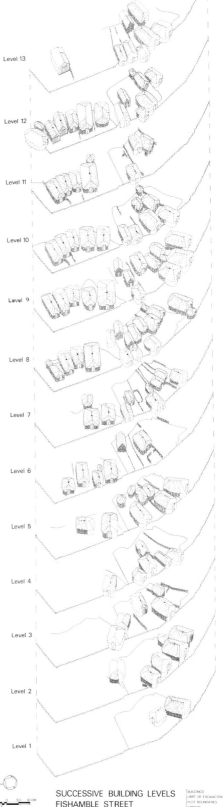

SUCCESSIVE BUILDING LEVELS
FISHAMBLE STREET

8

From Paganism to Christianity

Their pagan belief system was one of the signs
that made Vikings seem foreign to the Irish, whereas in
Dublin their descendants became Christians
with a difference

In most respects, Scandinavians of the Viking Age, as a people, were no more amoral than their Christian and Muslim contemporaries. Vikings as sea-pirates observed elements of a code of honour among themselves. Thus the swords of overlords and sacred arm-rings were used for oath-taking ceremonies. One such ring, dedicated to the pagan god Thór, was confiscated from the Dublin Norsemen by the high king, Máel Sechnaill mac Domnaill, in 995. This was an act akin to stealing a holy relic. Rather like that of later Christian knights (Latin *milites*), the Viking code of conduct was a warrior's code, which took little or no account of those who were not warriors. Monks and nuns, as well as ordinary men, women and children, might be killed or injured without compunction because they were not part of the warrior ethos. Equally, on the eve of the Viking Age, Charlemagne's Frankish armies butchered thousands of Saxons who resisted conversion to Christianity. Carolingian aggression south-west of their frontier was probably one reason why Danes were stirred into action in the early ninth century.

Pagan Gods and Goddesses

There is a famous description of a heathen temple that is said to have existed in the eleventh century at Old Uppsala in Sweden. The writer, Adam of Bremen, was himself a Christian and was hostile towards the continuing practice of heathenism across the Baltic Sea. In this temple, representations of three chief gods were honoured – Óðin, Thór and Frey. Centuries earlier, pagan Angles and Saxons had worshipped a similar trilogy of Germanic gods, whose names are still preserved in the English language as Woden's day (Wednesday), Thunor's or Thór's day (Thursday), and Fríg's day (Friday).

According to Adam of Bremen's account, an image of the god Thór was central to the temple's tableau. Thór was regarded by all Scandinavians as the most powerful of their pantheon of gods, being linked to elemental forces such as thunder, lightning, wind and rain. His symbol was a huge hammer, sparks from which were seen as lightning bolts. Even today, the German word for Thursday is

Burial mounds of pagan kings and the later Christian church at Old Uppsala, Sweden. The enormous size of these mounds is a reflection of social status. The heathen sacred grove and temple were replaced by the first church c. 1100.

Left: Silver Thór's hammer from the Skåne district of southern Sweden, 5.1 cm in length, made from two sheets of silver with a plain back and an elaborately decorated front, and dated c. 1000.

Centre: Bronze figurine of Óðin from Linby, Skåne. In Norse mythology Óðin rode around on an eight-legged horse called Sleipnir, the 'slipper'. In some high-status furnished graves in Scandinavia, one or more horses were buried alongside the dead warrior.

Right: Late Viking Age bronze figurine of the fertility god Frey from Rällinge, Sweden. Just 6.9 cm in height, he wears a conical cap and holds his luxuriant beard, a symbol of growth. Similar figurines were used as gaming pieces.

Donnerstag, 'thunder day'. Thór occurs frequently in place-names and in personal names, for he was identified socially with the common man. Ordinary farmers would make sacrifices of animals to him to ward off food shortages and disease. Amulets, possibly worn as charms against disease, have been found in Dublin.

Adam of Bremen also tells us that on one side of Thór in the temple at Old Uppsala stood an image of Óðin, who is often mentioned in Old Norse poetry as the god of war and of a select band of dead warriors. He was served by valkyries – female charioteers who conducted deserving warriors to an imaginary hall called Valhalla (the subject of a famous piece of music by the German composer Wagner). Óðin was also associated with two ravens, which flew high up and reported to him what was happening in the world, for he craved wisdom. Socially Óðin was identified with the elite of kings, chieftains and ordinary warriors, as well as with the poets who sang their praises.

The third major figure in the temple was Frey, a fertility god who was believed to be the ancestor of the ruling Yngling dynasty in Sweden. His symbols were a stallion and a boar, both noble and virile beasts. In an age of low population and high child mortality, the capacity of humans to reproduce themselves was greatly valued and a well-known figurine of Frey depicts him with an impressive phallus. Frey had a twin sister, Freyja, who also represented fertility and was the goddess joined by all dead women in their afterlife.

In addition there were many other gods with close Germanic parallels. Several Scandinavian place-name elements are linked with pagan cults, just like the occurrence of 'saint' in Christian ones. Examples are *–lundr*, 'grove', *–vé*, 'sanctuary' and *–hof*, 'farm' but also 'temple'. Pagan rites were usually conducted either in the open air or in a chieftain's hall. In contemporary Iceland chieftains commonly exercised priestly functions and were known by the specialised term *goði*, 'temple priest'. Interestingly this word is linguistically related to the English word 'god' and German *Gott*.

Pagan Beliefs

Among ordinary Scandinavians, festivals were held at the beginning of summer, after the harvest and at midwinter. The Old Norse word for the latter is *Jól*, which has gone into English as Yule. The pagan Yule lasted for thirteen days, the last coinciding with the Christian Epiphany, the day after Twelfth Night. There would have been great merry-making with tales of supernatural beings. On the eve of Yule, stores of food would be laid in and fresh ale brewed, at what some people still call Yuletide.

Early summer festivals were probably linked on occasion with forthcoming military operations at home and abroad. Animal sacrifices, processions, competitive games, and communal drinking and feasting all played a part. One Arabic visitor to Hedeby in the middle of the tenth century observed that householders would display the hides or skins of slaughtered animals on poles outside their homes to show that they had sacrificed to a god. In everyday life, personal talismans carved out of wood and other materials were carried or worn, especially in recognition of the three principal gods.

The god that brings us closest to the Viking mentality is Óðin. Blind in one

Left: Pendant or amulet from a female burial in Uppland, Sweden, dating from the ninth century. The figure, holding a sword and two spears, represents a priest rather than a warrior. This is the presumed origin of the horned helmet tradition.

Right: Heimdall blowing his horn to summon the gods to Ragnarök on a cross-slab from Jurby, Isle of Man. Heimdall was a deity with positive associations – beauty, brightness, wisdom and goodness – despite the tradition that his mythological father was Óðin.

Selection of troll dolls illustrating the Viking as a humorous icon with international appeal. In recent times, trolls are seen as good luck charms and purchased by tourists. The 'vikingisation' of products can add an extra appeal to consumers.

eye, his attributes were complex. He was thought to be cunning, demonic, pitiless and violent. Any sense of personal salvation to be derived from such a value system is impossible to gauge, but we may reasonably assume that the promise of entering Valhalla was at least equal to that of Heaven or Paradise for Christians. The cult of Thór, controller of elemental forces, may account in part for the almost reckless adventurousness displayed by Vikings as seafarers, while the cult of Óðin may have underpinned their equally renowned reputation as doughty fighters.

While they were in Valhalla, it was believed, Viking warriors would spend their time with Óðin fighting all day and feasting all night. They were being brought together in order to fight a final, apocalyptic battle against the forces of evil, known as Ragnarök. This word signifies 'world doom' and is akin to the Christian idea of doomsday. Just as the world was created, so would it come to an end and even the gods, including Óðin, would go down fighting. In his case, he would be swallowed up by his ancient enemy, the wolf called Fenrir, reminding us of the prevalence of these dangerous wild animals in the Viking world.

An Old Norse word that is still in current use, though in a totally modern context, is *troll*, a generic term for a giant, fiend or demon. Trolls were generally regarded as evil spirits inhabiting the wilderness, of which there was no shortage in Norway and Sweden in particular. One literary phrase (in *Færeyinga Saga*, the story of the Faroes) is *þykki mér þvi betr er fyrr taka troll við þér*, 'it seems to me that the sooner the trolls take you the better'. Nowadays, trolling has come to mean intentionally antagonising others online by posting inflammatory, irrelevant or offensive comments or disruptive content.

Óðin being attacked by the wolf Fenrir at Ragnarök on a cross-slab at Andreas, Isle of Man. Fenrir was the son of the treacherous god Loki and a giantess called Angrboda. Another child was the goddess or monster called Hel.

Preparing for the Next World

Pagan Scandinavians of the Viking Age believed in life after death, just like contemporary Christians. One important difference, however, was the belief that they could take earthly possessions with them into the next world, and hence the practice of being buried with possessions, sometimes only a single symbolic

object or a small selection of such objects. Broadly speaking, the richer you and your family were, the more you could take. What archaeologists call 'furnished' burials, that is, containing grave-goods for the afterlife, were a form of conspicuous consumption. Funeral rites could be an occasion for social display, as well as an expression of deeper personal and cultural affiliations.

We should always bear in mind that the commonest of all Viking Age grave-forms in Scandinavia itself was cremation. In most places the supply of timber was plentiful, while the hardness of the earth during winter would have made grave digging extremely arduous if

Left: Artist's reconstruction of a female burial in a chamber-grave at the trading settlement of Birka, Sweden, as it may have appeared when the grave was sealed. Women of high social status were dressed accordingly and in death accompanied by suitable artefacts.

Below: Composite map of the Kilmainham and Islandbridge grave fields. These graves and associated grave-goods came to light haphazardly over a long period of time.

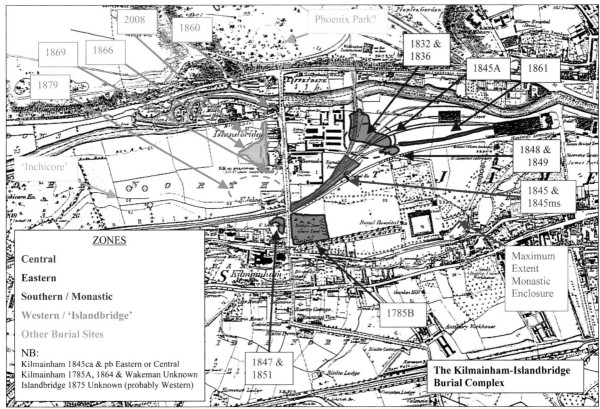

ZONES

Central

Eastern

Southern / Monastic

Western / 'Islandbridge'

Other Burial Sites

NB:
Kilmainham 1845ca & pb Eastern or Central
Kilmainham 1785A, 1864 & Wakeman Unknown
Islandbridge 1875 Unknown (probably Western)

The Kilmainham-Islandbridge Burial Complex

Maximum Extent Monastic Enclosure

Right: External and internal views of the better preserved of two oval brooches from the grave at Finglas. Dating from the *longphort* period, this is the only known example of its type where the raised animal heads have black glass eyes.

Two Dublin-type shield bosses from Kilmainham, west Dublin. Of the twenty-four bosses recovered from the whole burial complex, seventeen are of this type. Relatively standardised in design and size, they were probably made in a local workshop.

not impossible. The main exception in the Viking world was Iceland, where only one cremation site has ever been discovered archaeologically. Once the original light woodland had been cleared, timber was always in short supply. The reverse was the case in Ireland, where cremation may have been practised much as in the homelands.

This would help to account for the fact that, across the whole of Ireland, only 107 Viking graves have been identified. Of these, seventy-eight were male, thirteen female and sixteen unidentifiable by gender. Geographically the great majority have been found in the east, and neither Cork nor Limerick has produced any burial to date. Dublin has by far the largest concentration of furnished Viking graves, especially at the grave fields uncovered by railway workmen in the nineteenth century at Kilmainham and Islandbridge. With a grand total of eighty-one furnished graves, Dublin has yielded the biggest single assemblage of Viking graves anywhere west of Norway itself.

Despite the poor preservation of most Viking graves in Ireland and the general lack of skeletal remains, a certain amount can be deduced about pagan burial practices. Most such graves appear to have been shallow, earth-cut pits without the use of coffins. Grave orientation – the direction in which the burial faced – was not uniform. Individuals were probably buried fully dressed and animal remains, including those of horses, are rare in Irish Viking graves. The furnished burial rite was limited in Ireland mainly to the male elite, whose surviving skeletons reflect youthful robustness combined with early death. The solitary Finglas female, who was aged between twenty-five and thirty-five when she died, was comparatively mature.

The usual suite of equipment in warrior burials consisted of a sword, spear, shield and knife. Some weapon forms found in Ireland have been found nowhere else in the Viking world, especially shield bosses and spearheads, which were smaller than Scandinavian ones and perhaps adapted to Irish methods of fighting. One reason for variations in shield size could have been for recognition in the chaos of the battlefield. In the world of domesticity, dress-fasteners and jewellery seem to be equally divided between Scandinavian and Irish styles. Beautiful oval brooches, coming from ten or eleven graves, probably reflect the high social status of those particular women. They may have been heirlooms brought over from Scandinavia as cultural indicators.

Conversion to Christianity

The period when furnished burial was practised in Ireland has been defined as 830–930, after which it appears to have been replaced by a different cultural tradition. Geographically the Dublin concentration extended 8 km north–south and 10 km east–west. In other words, the Scandinavian kingdom of Dublin in the age of furnished burial was small and compact. And even in the *longphort* phase of Dublin's existence (841–902), elements of a mixed culture – part Norse and part Irish – were creeping in. Almost certainly, one of those cultural elements was Christianity.

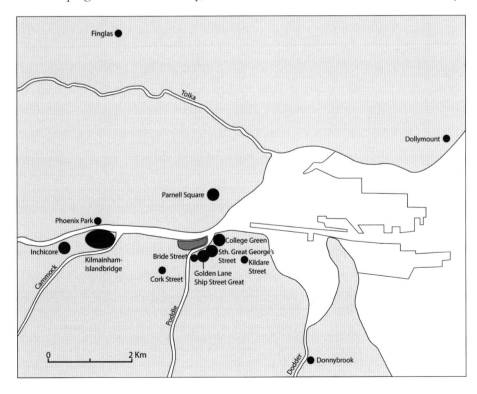

Viking graves and burial sites in the Dublin area. The majority were situated on the southern, Leinster side of the River Liffey. The Tolka may have served as the northern boundary of the early kingdom. The shoreline is medieval.

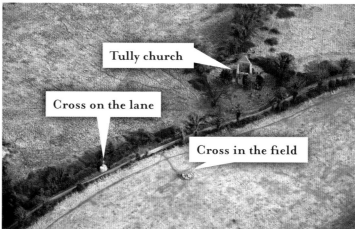

Left: Mould from Trendgården, Jutland, Denmark for making Thór's hammers and Christian crosses. Throughout the Viking world, paganism and Christianity coexisted. This mould may reflect the claim carved on the famous Jelling stone that King Haraldr Bluetooth made the Danes Christian.

Right: Aerial view of the ruined church at Tully near Cabinteely, south-east of Dublin. This church, associated with early bishops, was of some importance locally but was small in size. Its single enclosure measures 45 m by 30 m.

To ask when were the Vikings in Ireland converted to Christianity is to ask the wrong question. Unlike in Iceland, where a formal decision was made in favour of Christianity around the time of the first millennium, nothing like that ever happened. The evidence of furnished burial provides us with a vital clue: for Ireland as a whole, only fourteen percent are the graves of Viking women. In and around Scandinavian settlements in Ireland, the majority of the womenfolk must have been Irish and therefore Christian. We even know where some of them came from: in an early raid on Howth in 821, these Vikings took, according to the annals, 'a great prey of women'.

From the very start, then, Viking Dublin would have been populated by Irish-born women, as official wives, secondary (polygynous) wives and concubines, together with their offspring. The choice of burial rite would have fallen to them in most circumstances. The main settlement at Dublin would in addition have been surrounded by Christian cemeteries throughout the Viking Age, such as those that have been excavated at Castleknock and Cabinteely. Christian and pagan beliefs would have coexisted, though not necessarily harmoniously.

The great majority of ordinary churches in Ireland would not have contained much or anything of value. They could have continued to be frequented by most of the womenfolk and by those men of Scandinavian extraction who were attracted by the dominant religion of their adopted homeland. The pagan belief system persisted inside the *dún* of Dublin for a long time, hence the lack of church sites in the archaeological record.

The Irish annalists continue to refer to Scandinavians as non-Christians down to the third quarter of the tenth century, that is, to the time of Óláfr Kvaran as king of Dublin. His Christian faith may have been little more than

Map showing areas of Scandinavian influence and settlement in Scotland. By retiring to Iona, Óláfr Kvaran of Dublin was choosing a mixed Gaelic–Norse cultural environment. Only seven years later the monastery was attacked by Danish Vikings on Christmas night.

skin-deep, given that he was baptised as a young man in 943 at the behest of King Edmund of Wessex under military and political coercion, though he allegedly died as a penitent on the isle of Iona in 980. When Máel Sechnaill mac Domnaill captured Dublin for the second time in 989, the tribute in gold that he is said to have demanded from every householder was to be paid on Christmas night, which may be interpreted as a Christian slight on a still partly pagan population.

Drawing of a decorative copper-alloy belt buckle and strap-end currently on display in Dublinia's exhibition. These artefacts were excavated from the edge of a Viking burial in a robbing pit, dug to extract useful or precious items from a burial.

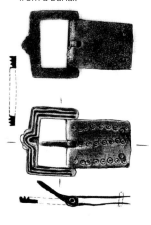

Drawing of the round tower of St Michael le Pole's Church dated to 1751. The radiocarbon determinations for the tower are some of the earliest in Dublin and the site may represent the location of an Early Christian monastic community.

FINDS BOX

Golden Lane, Dublin

Recent excavations have revealed evidence for early Viking activity around the southern perimeter of the black pool (now the Dubh Linn Garden) in the vicinity of the medieval parish church of St Michael le Pole. Remains of the church were identified and partially excavated by the Dublin Archaeological Research Team (DART) in 1981. The foundation of a round tower and a church and the remains of a medieval graveyard were preserved in situ, though no trace is visible above ground today.

Rescue excavations were subsequently carried out in 2005 on the corner of Golden Lane and Chancery Lane in advance of the construction of a hotel. A key planning requirement of the city archaeologist was the exemption of the site of the church and graveyard of St Michael le Pole from basement development and the preservation of the monument.

Nevertheless a total of 272 burials were excavated on the Golden Lane site in a halo outside the graveyard boundary wall. The burials have been dated to the early medieval period (*c.* 700–1200), including the Viking Age. The Irish grave morphologies include burials with eleventh- and twelfth-century stick-pins, confirming that Christian burial continued throughout the Viking Age without disruption.

Beyond the cemetery were a series of pits, a corn-drying kiln and five isolated burials. One of the outlying burials was interred with grave-goods that included an iron spearhead and a knife, two lead weights, and a buckle and strap-end. The skeleton is that of a stout adult male aged twenty-five years at the time of death. He has been interpreted as a pagan Viking buried just outside an Early Christian cemetery during the first half of the ninth century.

The site raises many questions about the relationship between the early church and both the Viking *longphort* and the later Hiberno-Norse town. The church and graveyard of St Michael le Pole will be preserved and commemorated as a landscaped open space in a future phase of the hotel development.

9

The End of the Viking Age

Historically it is generally more difficult to determine the end of an age than the beginning of one, the concept of a Viking Age being no exception to the rule

Archaeologists and historians tend to use different criteria from one another to classify past periods of time. Archaeologists are material-based in their analysis whereas historians are event-based. The biggest events in relation to Ireland, merely symbolic though they turned out to be, were the two expeditions by Magnus Barelegs, who was the king of Norway from 1093 to 1103. In the course of the first of these, in 1098, the king's overlordship of the Scottish isles was recognised; in the course of the second, in 1102–3, Magnus campaigned jointly with the high king of Ireland, Muirchertach Ua Briain, in Ulster, where he met his death in an ambush near the coast of Co. Down. As the Norwegian scholar Alexander Bugge pointed out long ago, this royal expedition 'assumed gigantic proportions in the imagination of the Irish, and grew to be an event that overshadowed all other contacts between the Norsemen and the Irish'. Verses were composed and a fictitious and romantic historical tradition was generated. Even so, *c.* 1100 remains internationally the most widely accepted termination of the Viking Age, although many Irish archaeologists still see the material culture of the Viking world continuing far into the twelfth century.

From Viking to Hiberno-Norse

For the purposes of this book, it will be helpful to divide the long period of time from *c.* 795 to *c.* 1100 into sections, at least as far as Dublin is concerned. In recent scholarship, a broadly recognised distinction is made between Viking Dublin and

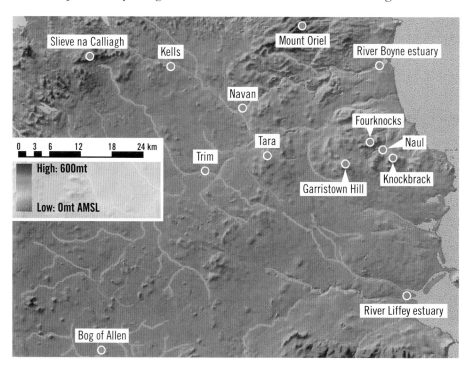

Hill-shaded model of Co. Meath showing the relation between Tara and Dublin. Long before the year 980 Tara had been abandoned as a habitation site, but was probably being used for inauguration to the high-kingship.

Hiberno-Norse Dublin. Though Irish influences were present from the start there came a point when a cultural balance was evident. This process was clearly not an event but occurred gradually during the tenth century.

A series of significant events that symbolise this transition took place in 980–1. In 980 the Northern Uí Néill high king, Domnall ua Néill, died and was likely to be replaced by an upcoming representative of the Southern Uí Néill, Máel Sechnaill mac Domnaill. In a time-honoured manner, Óláfr Kvaran led his Vikings on a major challenge to the newcomer, with allies from the Scottish isles. But at the battle fought at Tara, by then a mainly ceremonial site for royal inauguration, Máel Sechnaill was the decisive victor. One of Óláfr's sons was killed, his father surviving only to abdicate and to retire to Iona where he died later that year.

Probably early in 981, Máel Sechnaill besieged Dublin for three days and nights, captured it and released a large number of hostages. Some annalists, then or later, saw this event as the end of what they called the 'Babylonian captivity' of Ireland. No doubt this biblically inspired notion was an exaggeration, but thereafter the Dubliners rarely engaged in any military operation independently from Irish allies. Militarily they were not a spent force, but they came to be used, on land and at sea, as mercenaries serving more powerful native rulers. The new high king had set the tone for a new regime.

At this precise juncture a remarkable woman comes into the story. She was Gormlaith, a daughter of the king of the province of Leinster from 966 to 972,

Panel commemorating Máel Sechnaill's second capture of Dublin in 989, added to the rotunda of Dublin's city hall in the early twentieth century. The high king's army besieged the town for three weeks before it surrendered for lack of fresh water.

Murchad mac Finn. While probably still in her teens, she was married, for political reasons, to Óláfr Kvaran who was probably at least thirty years her senior. A son of that marriage was Sigtryggr Silkenbeard. After her husband's death on Iona in 980, Gormlaith became involved with Máel Sechnaill mac Domnaill, perhaps as a secondary wife.

Óláfr's immediate successor as king of Dublin was Glúniarainn Iron-knee, who was reportedly murdered in 989 by his own Irish slave while in a drunken stupor. Having captured Dublin again as an opportunistic political manoeuvre, Máel Sechnaill presumably arranged for the succession of a son of his Irish paramour, Gormlaith. Militarily, Sigtryggr's father, Óláfr, had failed decisively towards the end of his life and from 989 onwards the king of Dublin and his subjects can no longer be regarded as irrepressible Vikings.

The Battle of Clontarf

If in the Middle Ages the expeditions of King Magnus left a mark in popular culture, the equivalent for modern Irish people is the Battle of Clontarf, fought on Good Friday, 1014. The main reason for this has already been mentioned – *Cogadh Gáedhel re Gallaibh*, a Munster and an O'Brien literary product of the early twelfth century, when Brian Bórama's great-grandson, Muirchertach Ua Briain, was high king of Ireland. Since publication with an English translation in 1867, its image of King Brian – today usually called Brian Boru in popular

Panel depicting Brian Bórama addressing his army before the Battle of Clontarf, added to the rotunda of Dublin's city hall. By the early twentieth century this most dramatic battle of the Viking Age had become embedded in Ireland's national folklore.

discourse – of the Battle of Clontarf and of the Vikings in general has seized the imagination of many people, at home and abroad. The mindset of a medieval publicist and his audience has been transmitted across the generations, as if all were hearing what they wanted to hear.

The Battle of Clontarf should not be assessed, as it so often is, in isolation from other battles of the Viking Age. It was special in some respects, but far from being unprecedented. It struck contemporaries as being remarkable for a number of reasons, notably the casualty rate among the leadership on both sides and the dramatically tragic death of the high king. Yet Brian was not the first high king of Ireland to be killed by a Dublin-based army: in fact, he was the third. The same fate had befallen the Northern Uí Néill king Niall Glúndub in a battle fought at Islandbridge in 919 and the Southern Uí Néill king Congalath of Knowth, who was ambushed on his return from a plundering expedition into Leinster in 956.

At Tara in 980 another precedent was set, in that Óláfr had recruited, in advance, Vikings from the Northern and/or Western Isles of Scotland, just as his son Sigtryggr would do in the winter of 1013–14. Then the battle of Glenn Máma (probably near Newcastle, Co. Dublin) in 999 foresaw Clontarf in yet another way. This was an unsuccessful joint Dublin–Leinster encounter, fought outside the town, against an army assembled and led by Brian Bórama. Thus, in effect, not much that was genuinely new happened at Clontarf in the spring of 1014; only the scale was different.

In many ways the Battle of Clontarf was a family affair. In 1014 King Sigtryggr was Brian Bórama's son-in-law, while his mother Gormlaith was one of Brian's

An Irish warrior with spear and shield, from the Book of Kells. Irish soldiers appear to have been relatively lightly armed and protected but, in hand-to-hand fighting on foot, numbers counted and native forces scored many victories.

former wives (he had four in all). She and her brother Máel Mórda the king of Leinster, installed by the new high king in 1003, were now in alliance against Brian. Brian and Máel Mórda were both killed in the course of the fighting, whereas Sigtryggr and Gormlaith lived to tell the tale. (The myth that Brian was killed while praying in his tent derives from the *Cogadh Gáedhel re Gallaibh*.) On a family level, the real victor of the Battle of Clontarf was Sigtryggr Silkenbeard, who had succeeded in preserving his town from a Munster takeover.

One of the great ironies of the Munstermen's 'victory' on the field of battle in 1014 is that, for the next twenty-two years, Munster and Dublin were ruled by the half-brothers Donnchad and Sigtryggr, sons of the same mother Gormlaith. Donnchad's reign in Munster was often a troubled one, including as it did the murder of his half-brother Tadc (Muirchertach's grandfather) in 1023 and ending with his abdication and departure for Rome, where he died in 1064. Fifty years earlier, in classical fashion, the Munstermen had won the battle but lost the war.

Hugh Frazer's painting of the Battle of Clontarf dating from 1826. King Brian oversees the course of the fighting from a tent pitched on rising ground while groups of men engage with one another and Viking ships await the outcome.

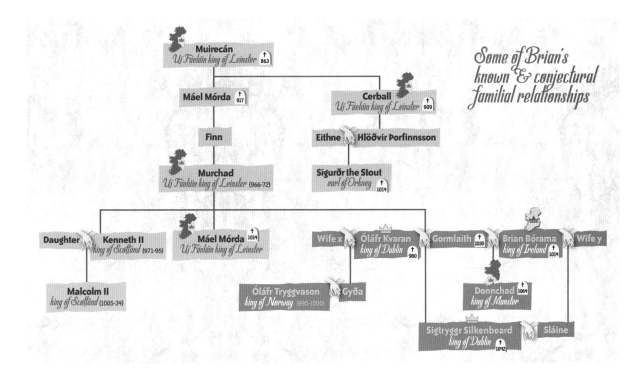

The Decline of Viking Power

The stock myth surrounding the Battle of Clontarf is that, by his military prowess, Brian Bórama had saved Ireland from a Viking conquest. Yet nothing could be further from the truth. Vikings had been incapable of conquering Ireland, a land of many kings and therefore of many armies. They always lacked the means in terms of men and materials. Even when they were a military force to be reckoned with, as in 919, 943 and 956, the Dublin Norsemen had shown not the slightest inclination to try to conquer Ireland.

Between 917 and 1014 at least twenty-five military engagements were fought in Ireland by the Dublin-based Norsemen, sometimes with Irish allies, including the Battle of Clontarf. Of these they won only ten. This catalogue of military defeats for the Dublin Norsemen is an impressive witness to resistance by the Irish. That resistance may have lacked the co-ordinated efforts of the peoples of Wessex and of English Mercia to defend their territory and then, in the second decade of the tenth century, to conquer Danish England as far north as the River Humber, but it was nevertheless effective.

Even more striking than victories on the field of battle was the series of Irish attacks on Viking Dublin itself. Between 936 and 1013 inclusive there were

Genealogical table showing some of the complex family relationships surrounding Brian Bórama. King Sigtryggr Silkenbeard was both Brian's stepson and son-in-law, while through his mother Gormlaith he was also the half-brother of Brian's successor as the king of Munster.

Raids by Dublin Norsemen and battles fought against Irish armies, 917–1014, the open circles indicating uncertain sites. Raiding was concentrated on a swathe of territory in Brega and northern Leinster, which also saw the greatest number of military encounters.

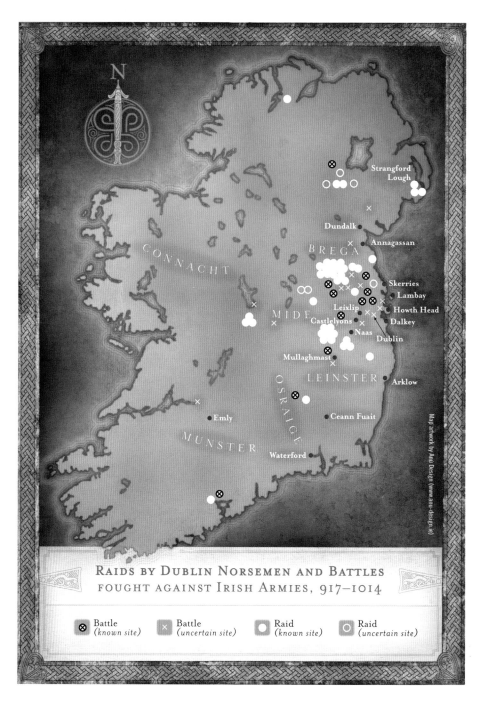

RAIDS BY DUBLIN NORSEMEN AND BATTLES
FOUGHT AGAINST IRISH ARMIES, 917–1014

⊗ Battle (known site)   ✕ Battle (uncertain site)   ◉ Raid (known site)   ◎ Raid (uncertain site)

Map artwork by Anu Design (www.anu-design.ie)

at least thirteen attacks on the *dún* of Dublin, most of them successful. Their leaders were usually reigning high kings, sometimes accompanied by allies. By the time of Brian Bórama's own capture of Dublin in the first days of the year

Map of Scandinavian
place-names in part of
north-western England.
Meols was a beach market
with a long trading history,
at which numerous ringed
pins and other Viking Age
artefacts have been found.
Dublin exiles settled in
Wirral in the early
tenth century.

Meols

WIRRAL

0   Km   20

SCANDINAVIAN PLACE-NAMES IN PART OF NORTH-WESTERN ENGLAND

● Habitative names   ○ Topographical names

Bank 2, first phase, at
Wood Quay, mid-tenth
century or earlier. This
defensive structure was
stabilised at its core by
a post-and-wattle fence
against which earth and
gravel were heaped.
Later, mortised planks
were placed on the
forward slope.

1000, following on from his victory at Glenn Máma, the Vikings of Dublin had effectively been brought to heel. Much of the credit for so doing should be accorded to Máel Sechnaill mac Domnaill and the men of Meath, who subdued the Dubliners on several occasions.

The converse of all of this is that Viking military power was replaced by Hiberno-Norse economic power. In the Icelandic sagas Dublin features as a major trading centre. Fragmentary documentary evidence and other clues suggest that Dublin had two main trading partners in England. One was Chester, the natural port for the north-west and north-west midlands, where several moneyers operating in the tenth and eleventh centuries had Gaelic names, implying links across the Irish Sea. The other was Bristol, the equivalent for the south-west and south-west midlands, which developed as a new port in the

eleventh century, a prime component of its trading activities being slaves. Economic power enabled the Hiberno-Norse population of Dublin to retain numerous elements of their Scandinavian culture, as the archaeological record shows. Analysis of ships' timbers show that Dublin's ships and boats remained in the mainstream of Viking tradition. Most spectacularly, the large vessel found in Roskilde Fjord in Denmark known as Skuldelev 2 has been interpreted as a longship built of oak from the Dublin region in the early 1040s. Norse influences are also represented by fourteen runic inscriptions on portable objects found in the Christchurch Place and Fishamble Street area of Dublin, whose general dating range lies between the late tenth and the mid-twelfth century. A further four have come from widely scattered parts of Ireland. The ultimate Viking legacy was cultural and economic rather than simply military and political.

Runic-inscribed scapula (shoulder blade), probably of a sheep, from Fishamble Street, late tenth century. These inscriptions appear to represent rueful observations about life.

Story-telling and the Sagas

Close-up of an illuminated initial 'G' for the character Gunnar on a copy of *Njál's Saga*. Sagas were copied in a style that was typical of Latin Christendom, this being the most popular of all.

In the collection of runic inscriptions found in the Christchurch Place and Fishamble Street area there are signs of both West Scandinavian and East Scandinavian speech, indicative of Norwegian and Danish strains in the population. The extent of Old Norse speaking is uncertain, but it has been suggested that a mainly lost saga dedicated to the deeds of Brian Bórama was composed, in Old Norse, in Dublin around the year 1100. What survives is the quite detailed, if partly fictitious, account of the Battle of Clontarf embedded in *Njál's Saga*, which dates from *c.* 1280 in the form in which we have it now.

Hinting at sorcery and the supernatural, this account of the great battle places King Sigtryggr in command of one flank of the rebel army before having him take to flight and his army with him. No mention at all is made of Máel Mórda, while Sigtryggr's supposed promise of his mother Gormlaith in marriage to Sigurðr, the earl of Orkney, is literary fantasy. As in the case of Shakespeare's history plays, the names of people and places in the sagas are often correct, but character and motivation were probably invented for literary purposes.

A suitable test-case is Dublin, which is mentioned casually in several sagas and in *Landnámabók*, the 'Book of Settlements' describing the early colonisation

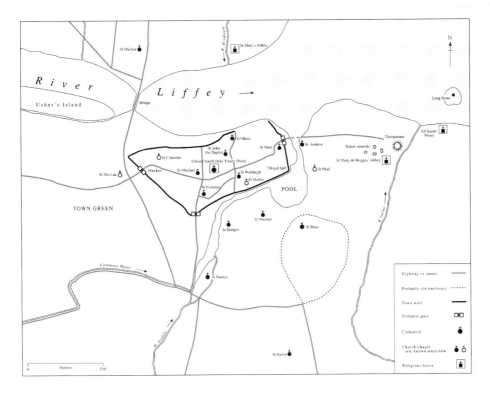

of Iceland. The latter also cites the territorial name Dyflinnarskíri (and variants) by which to refer to what the Irish called Fine Gall, the territory of the foreigners. Most of what is said or implied about Dublin is probably accurate: for example, that it was an important trading settlement, wealthy and normally approached by sea via the North Channel separating Ireland from Scotland.

Orkneyinga Saga, dating from around 1200, tells the story of the death of a latter-day Viking called Sveinn Asleifarson in a Dublin street. The townspeople

Iron Age broch (prehistoric round tower) at Gurness on the mainland of Orkney. The Norse presence is denoted by a female pagan grave. A complete Viking cemetery has been excavated across the sound, where a treeless landscape suggests limited agrarian resources.

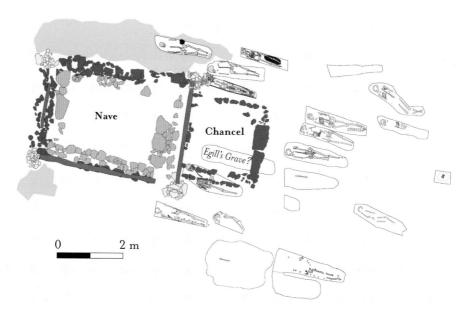

Plan of the church of c. 1000 at Hrísbrú. Egill Skallagrímsson is thought to have died c. 990 and was buried successively in a pagan mound, then in this church and finally elsewhere in Mosfell in the mid-eleventh century.

Nave

Chancel

Egill's Grave?

0   2 m

dig pits, cover them with branches, crowd Sveinn and his men into the trap and kill them there. None of this is likely to have taken place at the presumed time, the 1160s (just before the capture of Hiberno-Norse Dublin by the Anglo-Normans), but details such as streets, houses, town gates and an assembly of the leading men are likely to reflect reality.

The prevailing view among scholars is moving towards the idea that sagas are primarily a species of literature with a significant historical dimension. A dramatic archaeological demonstration has come recently from the chieftain's house at Hrísbrú first built around the year 900. This farmstead has been linked to *Egil's Saga*, to such an extent that details from the saga, along with advice from a local farmer, influenced the choice of where exactly to excavate. The result was an exceptionally well-preserved Viking Age combination of longhouse, pagan cremation site, stave church and Christian graveyard.

10
The Viking Legacy

The legacy of the Vikings was direct and immediate in the Viking Age itself, steeped in folklore later in the Middle Ages, and partly fictional in modern times

Making historical judgements involves perspective, both chronological and cultural. During the Viking Age, the perspectives of Vikings as sea-pirates, of the majority of Scandinavians in their homelands, and of those people whose lands were raided in, traded in or settled by Scandinavians were all different. These three activities – raiding, trading and settling – are quite distinct and should always be distinguished from one another whenever possible. A Norwegian sea-robber in Ireland was not the same sort of person as a Swedish river-trader in Russia. In the three

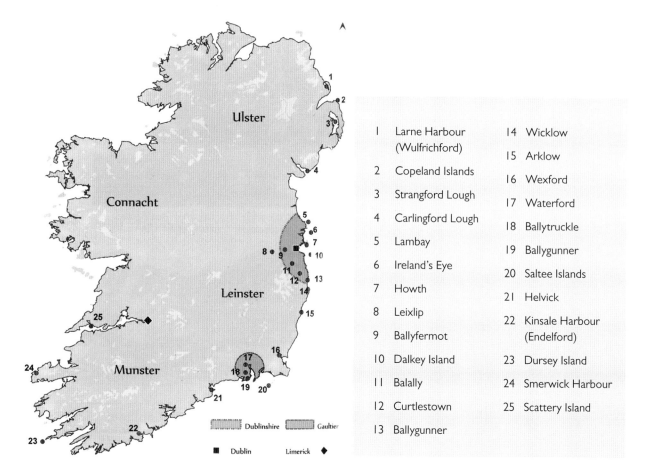

1	Larne Harbour (Wulfrichford)	14	Wicklow
2	Copeland Islands	15	Arklow
3	Strangford Lough	16	Wexford
4	Carlingford Lough	17	Waterford
5	Lambay	18	Ballytruckle
6	Ireland's Eye	19	Ballygunner
7	Howth	20	Saltee Islands
8	Leixlip	21	Helvick
9	Ballyfermot	22	Kinsale Harbour (Endelford)
10	Dalkey Island	23	Dursey Island
11	Balally	24	Smerwick Harbour
12	Curtlestown	25	Scattery Island
13	Ballygunner		

Map showing place-names of Nordic origin in Ireland. The territorial districts marked as Dublinshire and Gautier are purely notional and should not be understood as representing consistently maintained overlordships at any stage in the Viking Age. Boundaries fluctuated in practice.

Scandinavian homelands today, the Viking Age is the most famous part of their national histories, with the possible exception of seventeenth-century Sweden. The period *c.* 790 to *c.* 1100 saw the emergence in Scandinavia of the first national kingships, the first towns, the first local currencies; the conversion from paganism to Christianity and therefore the first churches and bishoprics; and extensive colonisation of the Faroes, Iceland, Greenland and, briefly, a small part of North America. An Irish and specifically a Dublin perspective is bound to be different from all of this.

Place-names and Languages

Outside Scandinavia, the best indicator of the short-term and long-term impact of the Viking presence is place-name distribution and place-name forms. This is a complex phenomenon and requires careful distinctions to be made. One of the most basic of these, and one that is crucial in Ireland, is between place-names that are purely Norse in form and those that are only partly so. While Norse names such as Leixlip were presumably accorded by the foreigners – the *gaill* as

The distribution of two of the principal place-name forms in Scotland. The elements *dalr* and *bolstaðr* mean 'valley' and 'homestead' respectively. Patterns of rural settlement of this kind were totally different from those in Ireland, characterised by coastal trading settlements.

Map artwork by Aña Design (www.ana-design.ie)

Place-names containing *dalr*

Place-names containing *bolstaðr*

THE DISTRIBUTION OF TWO OF THE PRINCIPAL PLACE-NAME FORMS IN SCOTLAND

Bolstaðr names
Bister, bster, bost, bus

Bolstaðr names
Boll, poll, etc.

the Irish called them – hybrid names such as Ballygunner (near Delgany) are just as likely to have been invented by those whose lands were being colonised.

Concentrations of both types of place-name differ enormously in north-western Europe. They are minimal in Ireland and south-western Wales, low in much of Britain and in northern France (Normandy), and significant in the Western Isles of Scotland (the Hebrides), the Isle of Man and parts of north-eastern England (the Danelaw). Maximum saturation by Norse settlers is apparent in the Northern Isles of Scotland, the Faroes and Iceland.

For Ireland, the place-name evidence suggests that sea-based trading was the principal Viking legacy, rather than rural settlement. There are a few fjord (*fjörðr*) names, notably Carlingford, Waterford and Wexford; two 'low' (*ló*) names reflecting low-lying land at the water's edge, Arklow and Wicklow; and more numerous coastal and insular names employed as navigational markers comparable with those along the northern and southern coasts of Wales. Hybrid names, part

Right: The Portmarnock
inlet at Baldoyle, Co. Fingal.
The place-name Baldoyle
is derived from *baile*,
'settlement' of Dubgall.
This personal name, 'dark
foreigner', belonged to
the half-brother of King
Sigtryggr Silkenbeard who
led the Dublin contingent
at the Battle of Clontarf.

The Gripsholm stone in
Södermanland, Sweden.
Runic inscriptions on
memorial stones are the
longest surviving Old
Norse texts from the
Viking Age itself. This
one, along the body of a
snake, tells of an ill-fated
expedition to the east.

Irish and part Norse, are found in the hinterlands of the main trading settlements. These probably arose from outward settlement in the late Viking Age or even from expulsion by Anglo-Normans in the twelfth century; they should not be interpreted as evidence for extensive Viking settlement. Thus, for instance, Balally in south Dublin (Baile meic Amhlaibh in 1179) was the settlement of the sons of an Óláfr who presumably acquired a farm there at some point in time.

Old English (Anglo-Saxon) and Old Norse are Germanic languages with similar syntax and vocabulary. Both languages use the special letters eth (∂) and thorn (þ) to represent voiced and unvoiced 'th'. It is commonly thought that Danish Vikings in England would have been able to make themselves understood by the native English: after all, the ancestors of many of the English themselves had originated in Angeln in Jutland. As a result, there was extensive borrowing into English from Old Norse, often in the spelling of words belonging to what linguists call Common Teutonic. Of the more abstract borrowings, the most striking is 'law' (Old Norse *lög*), reflecting a deep concern for legal procedures.

In sharp contrast, the Irish were Celtic speakers, at a considerable remove from speakers of Germanic languages. Initially there would have been simple exchanges until a sufficient amount of cultural immersion had taken place. There is a reference to the Irish term *gioc-goc*, which may be understood as pidgin Irish of the sort spoken by Vikings. Between two such distinct languages there was limited borrowing into Irish, mainly words connected with boating and fishing. By far the most telling loanword is *margadh*, 'bargain' or 'market', from Old Norse *marka∂r* (itself a borrowing from Latin), reflecting that most fundamental aspect of the Vikings' legacy in Ireland – raiders turned into traders.

Experimenting with the Past

As scientific methodologies and technology advance, our knowledge of Norse culture and heritage continues to increase. Isotopic analysis of bones and teeth is one such scientific method. Isotope oxygen values are related directly to the rain and groundwater consumed in childhood. These values differ across locations and can be used to pinpoint the area where a person grew up and even the movements of groups of people. The remains of four Viking warriors found in Dublin in 2003 were analysed using this method and revealed varied results. Two of them had grown up in Scandinavia, the other two in the Scottish isles.

Further discoveries about Vikings and their colonies have advanced through conservation and DNA studies. In the National Museum of Iceland are preserved the cheek and jaw of a young Viking Age woman discovered in 1938. Today's technology has been used to piece together her story – where she grew up, what she wore and how she was buried. Her burial is believed to have taken place between 915 and 925, while analysis of her remains revealed that she might have been Irish. In Sweden DNA results were used to create a life-size model of an individual from Sigtuna, 1.72 m tall and complete with blue eyes and blond-red hair.

In recent years, experimental archaeology has become a recognised academic discipline. At University College Dublin, the School of Archaeology has set up its

Left: Bone and flesh of a Viking Age woman in a jar of formaldehyde in the National Museum of Iceland. Her skin survived owing to a chemical reaction from two copper-alloy brooches buried near her face, which also stained her teeth green.

Right: Experimental archaeologist Stephen Fox demonstrating bow-making at Dublinia. The practical experience of harvesting and selecting suitable wood, of understanding the limitations of resources, and of working with ancient tools has led scientists to re-evaluate the evidence of our past.

A typical 'house fauna' type of beetle identified from floors in Viking Age Dublin and York. A surprising amount of information about the living conditions of ordinary people can be obtained by experts working at the coal face of experimental archaeology.

Centre for Experimental Archaeology and Ancient Technologies, using part of that university's extensive campus as the location for carrying out practical experiments. One of these, sponsored by Dublin City Council's city archaeologist, is a Viking house made only from materials and employing techniques that would have been available in the early eleventh century, during the lifetime of Sigtryggr Silkenbeard. Experiments are being conducted on questions such as light, temperature and smoke levels in the structure and how these would have affected the daily lives of the residents.

Animal bones, insects, plants, shells and wood provide clues to how our ancestors lived. Insects, in particular beetles, are sensitive to changes in environmental conditions and the forensic pathology of flies can establish a person's time of death and, where necessary, the original location of the body if it has been moved. It is the beetle that holds the key for archaeologists. Species survive in certain conditions, whether indoors and dry or outdoors and damp. In Viking Dublin beetles have pinpointed areas where food was stored, rubbish was accumulated and even where a toilet was situated.

Interpretation of the past and ways of understanding it take many forms. Re-enactment and living history have become popular in modern culture, with the result that large numbers of enthusiasts and academics have informed themselves by direct experience. Costumed interpreters equipped with an accurate understanding of the mechanisms of historical procedures bridge the gap between the present and the past on archaeological sites and in museums. At Dublinia, tour guides often wear a period re-enactment kit to demonstrate Viking Age activities such as bread making, fighting techniques and medical practices. Large-scale re-enactments such as that held in St Anne's Park in Dublin to commemorate the millennium of the Battle of Clontarf in 2014 have also demonstrated battle formations and tactics.

Popular Culture

The Vikings have been a major source of inspiration for both literature and the entertainment industry. One of the first popular novels with a Viking theme was *The Vikings of the Baltic* by Sir George Webbe Dasent, published in 1875, but more than eighty novels about Vikings have been written in English and no doubt many more in other languages. J.R.R. Tolkien drew upon his knowledge of Norse mythology when he created his novels *The Lord of the Rings* and *The Hobbit*. Many elements from Norse myths and sagas feature prominently in his stories, including dwarves, fire demons, magic, runes and, more recently, have inspired British writer Neil Gaiman to recreate his version of Norse sagas in his novel *Norse Mythology*.

Norse culture has also inspired digital and gaming technologies. Whether for education or just for fun, sophisticated computer-aided design and animation have recreated fantastical and idealised versions of Viking history. Immersive role-play or hack-and-slash artificial combat adventures, as in 'Vikings – Wolves of Midgard' by Kalypso Media, create a world where gamers travel through the realms of Norse mythology, killing creatures and freeing gods. Immersive digital experiences are also used to portray life in educational centres and museums. In the Mooesgaard Museum in Sweden, adults are invited on to a digital battlefield to experience the excitement and fear of being on an actual Viking battlefield. Closer to home, Waterford is hosting the world's first 3D Viking virtual reality adventure in a reconstructed Viking house.

Travis Fimmel as Ragnarr Loðbrók and Gabriel Byrne as Earl Haraldsson in the television series 'Vikings' created and written by Michael Hirst. Filmed mainly in Ireland, this mixes fact with fiction to great effect and is popular with audiences.

Viking art, artefacts and culture have had a big influence on the styling of costumes, props and even personal body art. The sets of Peter Jackson's Oscar-winning *Lord of the Rings* films are clearly influenced by Viking culture. Many other movies have featured Vikings as their main subject, including *The Vikings* starring Kirk Douglas, Tony Curtis and Janet Leigh (1958), and more recently *The Thirteenth Warrior* starring Antonio Banderas and based on a Michael Crichton novel (1999). The Oscar-nominated *Secret of Kells* by the Kilkenny animation studio Cartoon Saloon tells of a young scribe and his struggle against the impending Viking attack on his monastery (2009).

Cartoons and comics frequently feature Vikings. Perhaps this is an indication of just how deeply embedded in our subconscious, as well as our culture, they have become. For most children and adults, a Viking is as instantly recognisable as Mickey Mouse, despite the fact that Vikings are depicted in many different forms. These range from the amusing and hapless characters in Martyn Turner's cartoons for *The Irish Times* to the superheroes portrayed in the pages of Marvel comics. 'Vicious Vikings' make an inevitable appearance in several episodes of the *Horrible Histories* children's book series: in one, Thór searches for his stolen hammer while Asgot the Clumsy attempts to bluff his way into Valhalla in order to avoid going to Hell.

Vikings are also employed in advertising and marketing. In Ireland, the corporate symbol of Allied Irish Banks is a well-known example. The term 'Viking' is used by many organisations worldwide, from sports teams (Minnesota) to NASA's space probe to Mars. The prow and sail of a Viking ship were first used on the radiator badge of a Rover car in 1929 and before this the company had various images of a helmeted Viking as its logo.

More sinisterly, symbols for political extremists have been derived from Viking imagery. Such interest in the Vikings probably began in early twentieth-century Germany with the Thule Society, Thule being an ancient name for a distant land in the far north such as Iceland. This neo-pagan, nationalist movement had a high regard for all things Viking and believed that the Nordic peoples were descended from an Aryan race of superior beings. The concept of the blue-eyed, blond-haired Viking as an ideal model for Adolf Hitler's 'master race' can be traced to the fact that the Thule Society included Heinrich Himmler and many other high-ranking members of the Nazi Party – whose horrifying far-right ideology has not been fully eliminated from modern society.

Dublinia – a Vision of the Past for the Future

The legacy of the Vikings has gripped national and international audiences for centuries. For many, the iconic profile of a bearded and muscular warrior is no longer the default ideal of a Viking as more archaeological and historical information is retrieved. Whatever view we may adopt, there can be no doubt that Dublin and the Viking world are still with us and in good health. Dublin and Dublinia have long embraced this past, as has Waterford more recently with the development of its Viking Triangle of museums in the oldest part of the walled town.

Back in 1988 an experiment was pioneered in the historic heart of Dublin. This was the Irish Life Viking Adventure, sponsored by a successful life assurance company, featuring data from recent archaeological excavations in the city centre, the inspiration of one of the three site directors, Patrick Wallace. Life-size sets were constructed in the crypt of the nineteenth-century Roman

Scene from the Irish Life Viking Adventure. In this urban context, male and female characters featured. One woman is of high social status, wearing an elegant dress, brooches and necklace, while in the foreground there is a young domestic servant.

Catholic church of St Audoen and two teams of interpreters brought the whole experience to life. The interpreters, many of whom were actors, were trained by historian Howard Clarke to portray Vikings, or at least Hiberno-Norse town dwellers, as accurately as possible: for example, to estimate time by looking upwards to the (invisible) sun. It was immensely popular with the general public as well as visitors to Dublin, capturing the imaginations of children who today bring their own families to Dublinia.

In the popular Irish mind, by far the most famous legacy of the Viking Age is the Battle of Clontarf. In practice it has proved difficult to eradicate the belief that, by his military victory, Brian Bórama saved Ireland from a Viking conquest. In recognition of the millennium of the great battle in 2014, residents of Clontarf arranged for the compilation and installation of a series of graphic panels along the strand (in effect at intervals along Clontarf Road) on the northern shore of Dublin Bay. Meanwhile, in more fictitious mode, tourists can take a trip for fun, wearing horned helmets, along city centre streets in an amphibious vehicle with Viking Splash Tours. The trip culminates in entering the water at Grand Canal Dock.

Re-enactment of the Battle of Clontarf in St Anne's Park, Raheny, Dublin, in 2014. This location on relatively high ground back from the shore of Dublin Bay may be where the Munster army assembled prior to the commencement of hostilities.

Dublin and the Viking World

Picture Credits

The authors and publisher would like to thank the following individuals and institutions for giving permission to reproduce images:

Aarhus University Press, p96 (left); Amber Books, p18; Andrey Armyagov, p17; ART Collection/Alamy, p118; Avaldsnes Project, p21 (top); Arni Magnusson Museum (AM133 fol 59v), p122 (bottom); The Ashmolean Museum, University of Oxford (AN1836 p.135.371 The Alfred Jewel, 871–899), p41; BAR, p94 (left); Matti Bergström/National Board of Antiquities, Finland, p73 (top right); Bibliothèque Nationale de France, p44 (left); Berig/Wikimedia Commons, p44 (right); Bluetooth SIG, p132 (left); The Board of Trinity College Dublin, pp23 (bottom left), 117 (bottom); Bridgeman Art Gallery, pp53–54; Bridgeman Images, pp55 (bottom), 106 (bottom); Britain Express.com, p123 (bottom); The British Library, p62 (right); The British Museum, p97 (left); Jesse Byock, Mosfell Archaeological Project, pp79 (below), 124; The City of Bayeux, pp28–29; City Hall Dublin/Dublin City Council, pp116–117; Stephen Conlin, p13; Crown Copyright HES, p36 (top); Simon Dick, pp79 (top), 112 (top); Simon Dick/Linzi Simpson, p25 (bottom), p26 (bottom); The Discovery Programme, p114; Steve Doogan/Dublinia, pp45 (top), 74; Ros Drinkwater/Alamy, p115 (top); Dublin City Council, pp101 (left), 126; Dublin City Council/Botanic Gardens, p80; Dublin City Council/Johnny Ryan, p26 (top); Jan Dunbar/Hilary Murray/BAR British Series 119, p84 (top right); Anne Engesveen/Aarhus University Press, p19 (left); John Fahy/Dalkey Photos, p57; Aisling Flood/National Museum of Ireland, p45 (bottom); Roberto Fortuna and Kira Ursem/National Museum of Denmark, p81; Stephen Fox/Dublinia, p129 (right); Ken Gillespie Photography/Alamy, p82; Royal Irish Academy, pp 46 (top), 99, 123 (top); Jon H/Jurby church, p105 (right); Michael Heffernan/National Museum of Ireland, pp98, 101 (right); Kirsten Helgeland/Museum of Cultural History, University of Oslo, p32 (top); Heritage Image Partnership Ltd/Alamy, p39 (right); Historic England, p23 (top); Stefan Holm/123rf.com, p128 (left); Eirik Irgens Johnsen/Museum of Cultural History/CC-BY, p66 (top); Thorsten Kahlert (©Marion Dowd), p87 (top two); Werner Karrasch/Viking Ship Museum, Roskilde, p37 (bottom); Douglas Lander/Alamy, p19 (right); Lennart Larsen/ National Museum Denmark, pp33 (top), 34 (bottom), 68 (left); Barry Lewis/Alamy, p15 (left); Claire Liston/AIB, p132 (centre); Margaret Gowan and Co Ltd/Kevin Weldon, p50 (top); Margaret Gowan and Co Ltd/J Sunderland, p50 (bottom); Michael Maggs/CC-BY-SA, p72 (left); Montague Heritage Services/Dublinia, p130 (right); Emma Mooney, p134; John Murray/National Museum of Ireland, p109; Rose-Marie Murray/Alamy, p106 (top); National Library of Ireland, p52 (top), 88 (all images); National Monuments Service, Dept of Culture, Heritage, and the Gaeltacht, pp69 (right), 93, 110 (right); National Museum of Cultural History, Norway, p75 (top); National Museum of Denmark, pp75 (bottom); 76 (top); National Museum of Iceland, p129 (left); National Museum of Ireland/Michael Heffernan, pp55 (top), 65; National Museum of Ireland, pp21 (bottom), 33 (bottom), 58 (bottom), 59 (all images), 60 (all images), 63 (all images), 66 (bottom), 67 (all images), 68 (right), 69 (left), 70 (all images), 71 (all images), 73 (bottom), 81 (top left), 84 (top left), 86 (bottom), 87 (bottom), 108 (all images), 121 (bottom right), 122 (top); J Nicholls, p96 (right); Katarina Nimmervoll/The Swedish History Museum, p20 (top); Karen Nolan, p30; Karen Nolan/Dublinia, p119; Nordjyllands Historiske Museum, p36 (bottom); Niamh O'Broin/National Museum of Ireland, p86 (top); JG O'Donoghue, p49 (bottom); Tadhg O'Keeffe/Christ Church Cathedral, p100; Olaf Olsen/Viking Ship Museum, Roskilde, p37 (top); Ordnance Survey Ireland/Government of Ireland (copyright permit no. MP0005413), pp83 (all images), 107 (bottom); Osprey Publishing, pp43, 48; Kim Petersen/Alamy, p47; picturesbyrob/Alamy, p103; Neil Price/Þórhallur Þráinsson, p107 (top); Eileen Reilly, p130 (left); RTÉ Archives, p34 (bottom); Ian Russel, p58 (top); Johnny Ryan/Dublin City Council, p115 (bottom); Linzi Simpson/Mags Gowan, p15 (right); The Swedish History Museum, p31 (right); Statens Historiska Museum, Stockholm, p104 (left); Stephen Saks Photography/Alamy, p90; Esa Suominen, National Board of Antiquities, Finland, p46 (bottom); United States Holocaust Memorial Museum Collection, Gift of John Bolton, p132 (right); Urnes Stave Church, Fortidsminneforeningen.no/Jon E Tamnes, p76 (bottom right); Viking Ship Museum, Norway/CC BY, p31 (left); VK Five Productions, p131; Kit Weiss/National Museum of Denmark, p52 (bottom); Werner Forman Archive, pp39 (left), 104 (centre and right), 105 (left); Werner Forman Archive/National Museum, Copenhagen, p110 (left); Werner Forman Archive/Universitetets Oldsaksamling, Oslo, pp32 (bottom left), 84 (bottom); Wikinger Museum, Haithabu, pp78, 94 (bottom); York Archaeological Trust, p72 (right).

The authors and the publisher have endeavoured to establish the origin of all images used, and they apologise if any name has been omitted.

Suggestions for Further Reading

Barnes, M.P., Hagland, J.R. and Page, R.I. *The Runic Inscriptions of Viking Age Dublin*. Dublin: Royal Irish Academy, 1997.

Bradley, J. (ed.) *Viking Dublin Exposed: the Wood Quay Saga*. Dublin: The O'Brien Press, 1984.

Brink, S. (ed.) *The Viking World*. London: Routledge, 2008.

Cameron, E. *Scabbards and Sheaths from Viking and Medieval Dublin*. Dublin: National Museum of Ireland, 2007.

Chartrand, R. and others. *The Vikings: Voyagers of Discovery and Plunder*. Oxford and New York: Osprey Publishing, 2006.

Clarke, H.B., Ní Mhaonaigh, M. and Ó Floinn, R. (eds.) *Ireland and Scandinavia in the Early Viking Age*. Dublin: Four Courts Press, 1998.

Clarke, H.B. and Johnson, R. (eds.) *The Vikings in Ireland and Beyond: before and after the Battle of Clontarf*. Dublin: Four Courts Press, 2015.

Comey, M.G. *Coopers and Coopering in Viking Age Dublin*. Dublin: National Museum of Ireland, 2010.

Duffy, S. (ed.) *Medieval Dublin I: Proceedings of the Friends of Medieval Dublin Symposium*. Dublin: Four Courts Press, 2000. (Series continuing to present.)

Fanning, T. *Viking Age Ringed Pins from Dublin*. Dublin: Royal Irish Academy, 1994.

Forte, A., Oram, R. and Pedersen, F. *Viking Empires*. Cambridge: Cambridge University Press, 2005.

Geraghty, S. *Viking Dublin: Botanical Evidence from Fishamble Street*. Dublin: Royal Irish Academy, 1996.

Graham-Campbell, J. *The Viking World*. London: Frances Lincoln Publishers, 1980.

Graham-Campbell, J. and others (eds.) *Cultural Atlas of the Viking World*. Abingdon: Andromeda Oxford, 1994.

Grant, J. *An Introduction to Viking Mythology*. London: Apple Press, 1990.

Griffiths, D. *Vikings of the Irish Sea: Conflict and Assimilation AD 790–1050*. Stroud: History Press, 2010.

Halpin, A. *Weapons and Warfare in Viking and Medieval Dublin*. Dublin: National Museum of Ireland, 2008.

Harrison, S.H. and Ó Floinn, R. *Viking Graves and Grave-goods in Ireland*. Dublin: National Museum of Ireland, 2014.

Healey, T. *Life in the Viking Age*. London: The Reader's Digest Association, 1996.

Heckett, E.W. *Viking Age Headcoverings from Dublin*. Dublin: Royal Irish Academy, 2003.

Johnson, R. *Viking Age Dublin*. Dublin: Town House, 2004.

Konstam, A. *Historical Atlas of the Viking World*. London: Mercury Books, 2005.

Lang, J.T. *Viking Age Decorated Wood: a Study of its Ornament and Style*. Dublin: Royal Irish Academy, 1988.

Larsen, A.C. (ed.) *The Vikings in Ireland*. Roskilde: The Viking Ship Museum, 2001.

Murray, H. *Viking and Early Medieval Buildings in Dublin*. Oxford: British Archaeological Reports, 1983.

Roesdahl, E. and Wilson, D.M. (eds.) *From Viking to Crusader: the Scandinavians and Europe 800–1200*. Uddevalla: Bohusläningens Boktrycheri AB, 1992.

Russell, I. and Hurley, M.F. (eds.) *Woodstown: a Viking Age Settlement in Co. Waterford*. Dublin: Four Courts Press, 2014.

Sheehan, J. and Ó Corráin, D. (eds.) *The Viking Age: Ireland and the West. Papers from the Proceedings of the Fifteenth Viking Congress, Cork, 18–27 August 2005*. Dublin: Four Courts Press, 2010.

Simpson, L. *Director's Findings: Temple Bar West*. Dublin: Temple Bar Archaeology, 1999.

Valante, M.A. *The Vikings in Ireland: Settlement, Trade and Urbanisation*. Dublin: Four Courts Press, 2008.

Wallace, P.F. *The Viking Age Buildings of Dublin*. (Two parts.) Dublin: Royal Irish Academy, 1992.

Wallace, P.F. *Viking Dublin: the Wood Quay Excavations*. Dublin: Irish Academic Press, 2016.

Index

St Michan's Church

Church Street

Greek Street

St Michan's Street

Arran Street

Capel Street

Red LUAS Route

Red LUAS Route

Abbey Street Upper

Chancery Street

Mary's Abbey

Hammond Lane

Charles Street W.

Capel Street

Strand Street Gre

Church Street

Chancery Place

Arran Street E.

Ormond Quay Lo

Ormond Place

Ormond Quay Upper

Inns Quay

Ormond Quay Upper

R i v e r

Grattan Bridge

Father Mathew Bridge

Wellington Q

O'Donovan Rossa Bridge

Essex Quay

Merchant's Quay

Wood Quay

Exchange Street Lower

Essex Street

Lower Bridge Street

Essex Street West

Crane Lane

Dublin City Council

Fishamble Street

Parliament Street

Cook Street

Cook Street

9

Winetavern Street

10

5

Exchange Street Upper

Wood Quay Venue

Lord Edward Street

City Hall

St Audoen's Church

7

Castle Street

Dublin Castle

4

Cornmarket

3

High Street

1

Back Lane

Dublinia

Christchurch Place

6

Werburgh Street

12

8

Lamb Alley

2

Francis Street

Back Lane

Patrick Street

Christchurch Place

Ship Street Little

Dean Swift Square

Ross Rd

Ross Rd

Bride Street

11

VIKING DUE

1 Castle Street   4 Cornmarket   7 Christchurch Cathedral   10 Wood Quay Venue

2 Christchurch Place   5 Fishamble Street   8 Lamb Alley   11 Ship Street Little

3 High Street   6 Werburgh Street   9 Cook Street   12 Dubh Linn Garden

LUAS Route

North Lotts

Eden Quay

Strand Street Great

Liffey Street Lower

Bachelors Walk

O'Connell Bridge

Burgh Quay

Swifts Row

Ormond Quay Lower

Aston Quay

D'Olier Street

L i f f e y

Green LUAS Route

Westmoreland Street

Ha'penny Bridge

Fleet Street

Site of the
Long Stone

17

Millennium Bridge

Aston Place

Fleet Street

College Street

Temple Bar

Eustace Street

Cope Street

Anglesea Street

College Green Area

Trinity College

Temple Lane S

Crow Street

14 **15**

Eustace Street

Temple Bar

*Hoggen Green
Burial Mounds*

Dame Street

Dame Street

Trinity Street

*Site of Thingmót
(Assembly Place)*

Dame Street

Dame Lane

16

St. Andrew's Street

Suffolk Street

*Direction to National Museum
of Ireland (Kildare Street)*

Exchequer Street

Wicklow Street

South Great George's Street

Grafton Street

Nassau Street

Nassau Street

Drury Street

William Street

Coppinger Row

Johnson's Court

Grafton Street

Duke Street

Green LUAS Route

Nassau Street

Fade Street

13

Map artwork by Anú Design (www.anu-design.ie)

N – A GUIDE

e of Viking Burials   **16** Site of Thingmót
ggen Green   **17** Site of the Long Stone
ial Mounds

1 **4**
2 **5**   *Hiberno-Norse
Streets*
3 **6**

8 **10**
9 **11**   *Hiberno-Norse
Walls c. 1100*